ANDY WARHOL

AND THE CAN
THAT SOLD THE WORLD

ANDY WARHOL

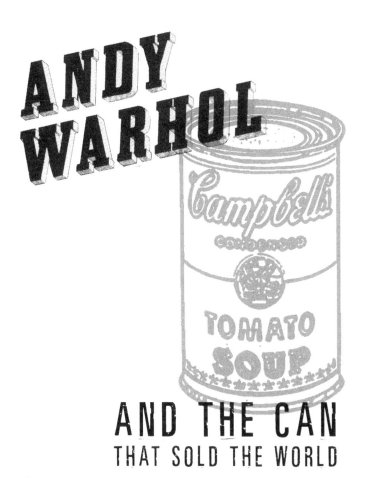

AND THE CAN
THAT SOLD THE WORLD

GARY INDIANA

BASIC
BOOKS

A MEMBER OF
THE PERSEUS BOOKS GROUP
NEW YORK

Published by Basic Books,
A Member of the Perseus Books Group

Books published by Basic Books are available at special discounts for bulk purchases in
the United States by corporations, institutions, and other organizations. For more information, please contact the Special Markets Department at the Perseus Books Group,
2300 Chestnut Street, Suite 200, Philadelphia, PA 19103, or call (800) 810-4145,
ext. 5000, or e-mail special.markets@perseusbooks.com.

Designed by Jeff Williams

Library of Congress Cataloging-in-Publication Data
Indiana, Gary.
    Andy Warhol and the can that sold the world / Gary Indiana.
        p. cm.
    ISBN 978-0-465-00233-7 (alk. paper)
    1. Warhol, Andy, 1928–1987. Campbell's Soup cans. 2. Warhol, Andy, 1928–1987—
Criticism and interpretation. 3. Avant-garde (Aesthetics)—United States—History—
20th century. I. Warhol, Andy, 1928–1987. II. Title.

ND237.W353I53 2010
759.13—dc22

                                                        2009041684

10 9 8 7 6 5 4 3 2 1

FOR

MARY WORONOV

AND

CHARLES RYDELL

IT'S TOO HARD TO LOOK IN THE MIRROR.
THERE'S NOTHING THERE.

ANDY WARHOL
interview with Jordan Crandall,
Splash, No. 6 (1986)

CONTENTS

PREFACE

LOSE TO A QUARTER-CENTURY AFTER HIS DEATH, Andy Warhol continues to evoke ambivalence and polarized appraisal, despite his work's almost surreal financial appreciation.

Cultural conservatives disparage him and blame him for nearly everything appalling in American culture; at a different extreme, virtually everything he produced is lauded as prescient, masterful, and, especially, prophetic—and there are also those who think both judgments are true.

There is a museum devoted to his work in his hometown of Pittsburgh. A foundation that bears his name distributes millions for worthwhile artistic endeavors. A catalogue raisonné, years in the making and still incomplete, may dispel many confusions and myths concerning the circumstances in which Warhol's vast oeuvre was generated. Yet the mythmaking porosity of Warhol's enterprise will certainly retain its usefulness in the perpetual revision of the kind of history generated by rumor, gossip, and word of mouth—the history that occurs before it becomes history in the sedimented, old-fashioned sense.

In the twentieth century, perhaps only Picasso left a comparably prodigious and variegated body of work, and therefore there will always be more to say about it. No one will ever get the final word on Andy Warhol. Like many people who came of age during the peak of the Warhol phenomenon, I considered him a brilliant provocateur, an artist of genius whose personality, as much as his art, exposed the vapid conformity, sexual repressiveness, and crass commercial values of American culture that prevailed during my childhood; like many, I read into Warhol's ongoing enterprise a satirical contempt for the banality of that culture and its norms. That enterprise had, at first, a decidedly marginal character, appealed to a special kind of minority sensibility, and was valued precisely because of its "countercultural" insouciance. Later, however, as Warhol's work achieved mainstream acceptance and the artist became synonymous with the culture of celebrity-for-its-own-sake and financial success as the measure of any artistic activity's value, I became far less admiring of Warhol's achievement and much more critical of Warhol's career as it played itself out—without, I must add, ceasing to marvel at the audacity of his early work and his preternatural productivity or to appreciate the vast range of cultural practices and social changes, both baleful and appealing, that have been, to one degree or another, inspired by Warhol's example.

If he had simply been a famous artist with a flashy personality, like Picasso, there would no doubt be firmer anchorage for assertions of intention, the parsing of works into clearly defined "periods," and less skepticism about the value of the artist's work overall.

In the case of Andy Warhol, the personality is one of implacable ambiguity, deliberate mystification, and a pose of complete detachment from his own work, a tyrant of passivity. Picasso began from a traditional "fine art" practice of painting that he revolutionized with Cubism and subsequent innovations. Warhol, who was trained in commercial art and first achieved eminence in that field, demolished the critical and perceptual boundaries separating "fine" and "applied" art, most memorably by exhibiting a series of *Campbell's Soup Can* paintings in an art gallery.

Although hand-painted, the *Soup Cans* had the look of their industrially reproduced models. Warhol soon went further, applying the methods of mechanical reproduction to painting, including later versions of the

Soup Cans; he extended this industrial model of production to sculpture and the whole gamut of customarily "handmade" works of art, glorifying the banal artifacts of American consumer culture and its icons of celebrity. The *Soup Cans*, at first widely dismissed as the ultimate cynical gimmick, were soon recognized as the first shots of a total revolution in American culture.

These pictures emitted no "aura," no irreplaceable uniqueness, none of the qualities traditionally thought to emanate from works of art. What they conveyed was the enshrinement of a trademark commodity that the artist himself had had to swallow every day for lunch as a child—a kind of condensed regurgitation of what "America" meant to Andy Warhol.

Yet whether the *Soup Cans*, and the staggering quantity of works that followed, signified contempt or reverence, love or loathing, a mixture of feelings or an absence of any feelings at all, could not be gleaned from the paintings themselves. And the artist had, by the time they were shown, perfected a laconic and distancing persona that confounded any definition and presented itself to the public as a glacial enigma.

This enigmatic quality, which made Warhol a celebrity, infused all his work with a kind of empty secret. It was there for others to interpret; the brilliantly terse aphorisms he coined about himself and his work, the interviews in which he claimed that other people did all his paintings for him, the exhibitionists he collected as a sort of protective gang around him, created a vast field of legend that steadily multiplied the value of everything he made.

Careers have been minted from inventories of innocently and not-so-innocently repeated, thousand-told anecdotes with dubious moorings in reality. The mind-numbing deluge of writings about Warhol includes factual slippages of every stripe, impossible-to-confirm stories, and, quite likely, facts that have been eclipsed by more interesting apocrypha.

We can each be one person's saint, another's bastard, a third's genius, and someone else's imbecile. Warhol was that rare individual who could be all these things, at the same time, to the same person. From the distance of an interested spectator, he certainly appeared to be that rarity to me.

PART ONE

Abjection and Epiphany

chapter one

THE BOY ON THE HILL

ONE

ANDY WARHOL CONTINUALLY REVISED AND MUDDIED his background. His contradictory self-inventions were often freely embellished by those who heard them, though now, in posthumous finality, his densely veiled life may look slightly less veiled.

Authentic copies of his birth certificate have appeared in publications. His birthplace was just plain Pittsburgh—not McKeesport, Pennsylvania, or Hawaii, or other places he sometimes claimed to have been born. Scholars can trace his movements from birth to his arrival in New York City, and, with considerably more difficulty, afterwards.

Born in 1928, Andy Warhola was the youngest of three brothers. Andy's parents, Julia Zavacky and Ondrej Warhola, married in 1909 in Ruthenia, a Carpathian sliver of impoverished villages, epidemics, illiteracy, and hapless geography in the path of incessant territorial skirmishes between neighboring countries.

Ondrej, who had already spent three years working in the United States, returned to America three years after their wedding. A baby daughter was born after his departure and died before Ondrej earned enough money to bring his wife to the new country.

Julia never entirely recovered from this child's loss.

Nine years passed before she could join Ondrej in Pittsburgh. There the couple produced three sons— Paul, John, and finally Andrew. The family lived in the Ruthenian ghetto known as the Hill, and its isolation resembled Ruthenia itself.

Descriptions of Andy's childhood evoke bravely maintained family cohesion in abject circumstances, with a father often absent, obliged to travel for his work for a company that transplanted whole houses from one place to another. Warhol later described his early home as the worst place on earth. On another occasion he remarked that being born was like being kidnapped and sold into slavery.

Ondrej died in 1942, when Andy was fourteen. Andy's father's dying ukase was that his savings be spent to start Andy in college: Paul and John would have to work to support the family.

Andy Warhol later said he barely remembered his father.

TWO

Superficially at least, the family appeared content to struggle with its lot. Its members may even have felt a contentment within a cycle of poverty mirrored in the families around them.

Only Andy, the problem child, posed any threat to the family's cohesive self-image. Yet this sort of sub-dural, intractable wound—inflicted by the excessive love and material favoritism that jangled the family's equilibrium, depriving Andy's siblings of their share of attention and care—may not have appeared as dramatic as it sounds.

Early on, Andy staked out special-child status among his brothers. His father's frequent absences left the elder Paul as the putative male head of the family, a role he fully assumed after Ondrej's early death.

Andy was the family's moody, tyrannical center-piece. The child had panic attacks and was prone to hysteria. He shaped weaknesses into weapons for rejecting anyone he didn't like and avoiding anything he didn't want to do. He manifested the estrangement and neediness of the gifted child, cursed and blessed with qualities foreign, magical, and possibly frightening to those around him. The misery of such a child, "kidnapped" into a Depression-era, uneducated family, is immeasurable. Regardless of the family's primal bonds of love, its inability to comprehend him and his inability to understand himself inevitably nurtured a degree of resentment and produced from the child sadistically impossible demands and intolerable behavior.

Andy refused to go to grade school after a black female classmate slapped him. Lonely Julia, with a shrewd peasant gift for sculpting permanent dependence, kept him home for two years while Ondrej was away, until brother Paul put his foot down. After a mild bout of malingering that Andy prolonged into a full month in bed, a neighbor friend forcibly carried Andy to school. Andy immediately suffered a histrionic relapse that kept him home for many months.

His real and imaginary illnesses, his pathological shyness, and his remarkable artistic talents intimidated the family menagerie into catering to his wishes. Cluelessness and anger must have accompanied the resource-draining sacrifices that were made to satisfy Andy's wants (like the dollar-a-day housecleaning jobs Julia took to buy Andy a $20 cartoon projector). These wishes could never be fully satisfied: gifted children are quite often incapable of happiness and can only be temporarily placated. What gifted children often want is idolatry rather than happiness.

We do have it on the artist's word, and that of his brothers, that the Warhola sons' childhood lunch unvaryingly included Campbell's soup and a sandwich—and that Andy got to pick the day's soup flavor.

THREE

Julia was maniacally devout. She brought Andy with her on daily two-mile treks from the Hill to St. John Chrysostom Eastern Rite Greek Catholic Church. The church's densely crowded-together gilded icons of saints and strict formal rituals probably had later echoes in Warhol's sanctifying portraits of Marilyn Monroe and other film stars, as well as the dramaturgy of the Factory, with its hierarchies of "Superstars" and its atmosphere of a travesty religion, where devotees "confessed" to a godlike camera and were "absolved" by inclusion in a community of dysfunction.

Described as a gentle, kind person, Julia undoubtedly was. But she was more complex than the blurred image of her captured in later years by Duane Michals's camera and the painting Andy made of her.

Pretty, funny, talented at drawing, and, until her last years, able to contain the melancholia that haunted her, Julia repined for the world of her childhood. She never truly left Ruthenia, it's been said; she lived very much in the mental world of her own childhood. The harsh conditions of that childhood, its cultural and material poverty, remained imprinted on Julia's mind in an alien country where she found everything familiar turned askew, and her fierce maternal instincts toward her favorite child were laced with panic. His difference from the norm made her overbearing and hypercritical, ferociously protective yet perpetually disappointed; while she sought to mold Andy in her own image, his nascent lack of "manliness," his manipulative spells of sickness and "feminine" methods of getting his own way, must have often stricken her with guilt and anger.

Julia's disproportionate attention on her Little Prince was entangled with contempt. The "holy terror" described in Bob Colacello's exemplary biography is the calculating crybaby and revered brat who evolves from coddled child into adult monster. Child Andy was mother Julia's tantrum-prone, acne-riddled, albino lion cub, smothered with attention and chocolate rewards when he completed pages of his coloring books. Yet Julia also told him that he was ugly, that his nose was too big, that he was nothing. Her pride in him warred with her envy: sins joined at the hip. Julia's psychic cannibalism—in every account her possessiveness amounts to this—was "well intended," yet devastating.

Julia shaped Andy into Nothing Special, and a Special Nothing. Warhol's acute sense of the void, many years later, would be the basis of his best art. His awareness of Nothingness, and his terror of it, were tenuously balanced by his lifelong Catholicism—a religion that instills the idea that anything can be forgiven if penance is made, forgiveness asked for.

FOUR

Three childhood "nervous breakdowns" are attributed to Saint Vitus' dance. These always occurred in summer months, when Warhol, rarely leaving his island bed, listened to radio serials, scissored paper dolls, crayoned coloring books, and played with a Charlie McCarthy dummy.

Radio was the murmuring hearth of the American home in the 1920s and '30s, acrackle with serials like *The Shadow* and, paradoxically, the wildly popular ventriloquism of Edgar Bergen. Warhol's fantasy fed on radio, comics, and *Photoplay*. He prized radio's Niagara of voices and sought it in chatty grade-school girlfriends; later he would replicate this torrent of talk by filming his loquacious Superstars—like Ondine, a flume of scathing wit fueled by massive amphetamine consumption, and Viva, who could engagingly drone for hours about her Catholic girlhood, her bizarre upperclass Irish family, and her sexual adventures, whether anyone was listening or not.

We don't know whether the chronically convalescent ten-year-old Andrew Warhola tuned in to Orson Welles's Campbell Playhouse productions of *A Christmas Carol*, *A Night to Remember*, *Theodora Goes Wild*, *Dodsworth*, and *Mr. Deeds Goes to Town*. It's unlikely that the supple, thunderous radio voice of Welles—an American theatrical legend at twenty-three—would have escaped the attention of a boy who collected $8 \times 10"$ autographed glossies of film stars and had adopted the mannerisms of his idol, Shirley Temple.

The Mercury Theater, launched by Welles and John Houseman in 1937, was an ambitious repertory venture in the spirit of Roosevelt's populist New Deal. Within a year, the company was offering, as *The Mercury Theater of the Air*, one-hour weekly dramas under the auspices of CBS, adapting literary works like *Treasure Island* and *Dracula.*

The Mercury's radio venture went south soon after it unintentionally spread panic throughout depressingly large, credulous regions of the United States with its dramatization of H. G. Wells's *The War of the Worlds.* During the ensuing scandal, the Campbell Soup Company picked up sponsorship of the Mercury's radio theater, allowing CBS to withdraw.

The Mercury Theater of the Air was soon reconfigured into *The Campbell Playhouse*, and this commercialization of Welles's arguably highbrow experiment in radio wreaked significant changes in the flavor of the fare being offered. Simon Callow, Welles's biographer, writes that the original ensemble's tone "was only occasionally reverential, more often blithe, high-spirited, dashingly dramatic. Not all of that was lost with the reinvention of the programme as The Campbell Playhouse, but it was a radically different animal, and it made of Welles a rather different animal, too."

The difference is notable when you compare the Mercury Theater broadcasts with the Campbell-sponsored ones. The latter, preceded by a ponderous Bernard Herrmann fanfare, lavishes several minutes on an announcer's deifying résumé of Welles's theatrical career, followed by Welles's own purple lucubrations over his costar—in the debut broadcast, Margaret Sullavan. As Callow describes it:

> This new tone, quite different from his Mercury manner: what would later become familiar as the manner of the chat show, but which in 1938 was about puffing. . . . The Welles of The Campbell Playhouse . . . was a significantly different person to the Welles of the Theater of the Air: master of ceremonies, celebrity, leading actor, salesman, he had become appreciably more a product of the image makers. . . . He has, above all, gone commercial, the selling of the sponsor's product and his own indistinguishable from one another; both indistinguishable from the selling of himself. The tone in which he extolls the beauty of radio as a medium is the same as the one in which he lauds the makers of Campbell Soup.[1]

Between segments of *Rebecca*, Welles gravely extolled the Campbell Soup Company's public-spirited virtu: "I know the Campbell kitchen, the Campbell soup, the Campbell men: their success is due to the human side of this business, its policy."

A notable feature of these commercials is a recurring theme of modernity—the modernity of the Campbell Playhouse's selection of "the finest of today's drama," blended with the modernity of rich, wholesome, possibly better-than-homemade tomato, vegetable, chicken, and other Campbell's soups whose preparation requires nothing more than a pot and a can opener. What could be more modern than getting dinner from a can?

Welles's metamorphosis from artist to celebrity entrepreneur prefigured Warhol's own. Like Welles, Warhol became as much the product he sold as the art he made. His ambition enlarged exponentially when he realized what unlimited success was available to him. Warhol didn't have Welles's hammy baritone eloquence; though far more familiar with "high culture" than he generally let on, Warhol cultivated a repertoire of exactly the opposite methods of self-presentation, starting in his college years. Like Welles, Warhol understood the power of silence, of the clipped riposte—even though his aggressive passivity couldn't have been further from Welles's cultivated image as bon vivant and raconteur.

The two artists also shared a mandarin dexterity in manipulating other people in the service of boundless ambition as well as the ability to set members of their entourages at odds with each other through well-placed gossip. Both also suffered severe late-career slumps they never fully overcame. And of course, Welles and Warhol both had a far from coincidental involvement with Campbell's soup: the merger of corporatism with art.

FIVE

As a child, Warhol exhibited precocious drawing skills and colorist ingenuity, and he had an insatiable appetite for movie magazines. He collected "personalized" autographed photographs of film stars as a child.

Andy's brothers Paul and John sold produce from a truck bed in flourishing Pittsburgh neighborhoods. Andy tagged along, pitched in, and earned extra quarters selling dashed-off portraits of the customers. Turning art into cash was an early lesson in capitalism and the power of flattery.

Warhol's formal art training began early, at age nine, when he was accepted for Saturday morning classes at the Carnegie Museum. These opened Andy's perspective to a realm of finer things, brought him in contact with other students from other rungs of the social ladder, and equipped him with the technical skills he would need in his later career.

After graduating from Shenley High in the Oakland section of Pittsburgh, Warhol enrolled in the

School of Fine Arts at the Carnegie Technical Institute, a technical college established to educate the children of steelworkers that eventually became present-day Carnegie Mellon University.

He was several years younger than the other students, many of whom were veterans attending college on the GI Bill. Nevertheless, by all accounts Andy flourished in his new environment. Andy's nephew, Jamie Warhola, observed:

> I would think that would be really intimidating to be up against all those GI jocks, yet Andy became comfortable enough amongst his heterosexual peers to outdo them on assignments. In a way, I think it was like boot camp in the artworld for him. He may have had this soft-spoken, quiet awkwardness on the personality side but on the artistic playing field he was aggressive and tough. . . . As for his fellow students, they generally grew to love him and were always looking forward to his solutions because of how great they always were and how he was able to create a little havoc for the teachers.[2]

At Carnegie, Warhol adopted the blotted-line technique of wet-pressed drawing, familiar from the work of Ben Shahn, and refined this method to produce multiple versions of the same image—a technique he used throughout his commercial art career.

Despite his initial shyness and passivity, Andy soon manifested eccentricities and mannerisms that suggested homosexuality. This wasn't particularly scandalous in art school, and Warhol seems not to have been sexually active at the time, but simply, on occasion, overtly odd in his self-presentation. He once appeared at a party with his hair dyed green. Schoolmate Betty Ash thought "he was trying to look like a woman in a painting by Matisse," but biographer Victor Bockris astutely thinks it likely that Warhol was imitating the eponymous victim-protagonist of Joseph Losey's 1948 film *The Boy with Green Hair*.

His work at Carnegie was sometimes strangely, defiantly unconventional; Andy produced several dog paintings inspired by instructor Balcolm Green's Russian wolfhound. One showed a woman nursing a baby dog. It was included in a small student exhibition, but then removed at the insistence of a technical-resources instructor.

For the 1949 exhibition of the Pittsburgh Associated Artists, Andy submitted a controversial canvas informally dubbed *Nosepicker* but actually entitled *The Broad Gave Me My Face, but I Can Pick My Own Nose*. The painting, reminiscent of works by George Grosz, depicts a boy with a finger jammed up one nostril; the exhibition jury, which happened to include Grosz, was divided about whether the work was "important" or dreadful. The picture was finally rejected, but earned Andy notoriety—it was, according to Bockris, "Andy's first *succès de scandale*."

chapter two

LEAP OF FATE

O N E

IN THE MONTHS BEFORE GRADUATION FROM CARNEGIE IN 1949, Warhol equivocated about his future plans. He considered becoming a high school art teacher and even applied unsuccessfully for such a job at an art school in Indiana; he was hesitant to move to New York, but was finally prodded to do so by his friend and collaborator Philip Pearlstein's determination to go there. They both faced daunting odds in the city they'd visited a year earlier, though Warhol had been gutsy enough on that occasion to show his portfolio to Tina Fredericks, the art director of *Glamour*; she had promised him work. Earlier Carnegie alumni already settled in New

York offered contacts in the commercial art world. But there was a considerable gap between magazine illustration and the world of "fine art" that both Pearlstein's and Warhol's ambitions would have to breach.

From scattered beginnings in the 1930s, New York–based "modernist" art gained heft and traction during and after World War II. Like many art movements in Europe throughout the first half of the century, it initially roused interest, pro and con, within an art-centered elite, gradually became known to a wider public, and then became the subject of mass publicity. "The New York School," "Abstract Expressionism," or "Action Painting," as it would variously be known, finally received the institutional embrace of the people whose business it was to shape public perception and bestow financial value on works of art.

In the contemporary understanding of the term, there was no "art world" in the United States before 1945. The first decades of the twentieth century produced outstanding American artists influenced by European modernism, among them Florine Stettheimer, Max Weber, Arthur Dove, Stanton Macdonald-Wright, Charles Demuth, Stuart Davis, and Marsden Hartley. The work of these artists received limited exposure, negligible in comparison with the reception given to the bucolic realism of Norman Rockwell and similar celebrants of insular, basically rural and small-town visions of America. The latter, which didn't represent any "movement," were painted in a nonstyle of illustrational kitsch in which "ordinary people" recognized the platitudes and ideals of an agrarian country, its moral homilies, its wholesome and ever-renewed innocence.

The country had no lack of imaginative, formally inventive artists in the 1920s and '30s, but they had no viable art system for marketing their work. Many artists survived the Depression years by working in Roosevelt's Works Progress Administration (WPA), painting murals and executing other public art for the government, but the war effort dried up funding for this resource. Artists whom the WPA had enabled to hone their talents found themselves with studios full of unsaleable art.

This situation changed for a fraction of formerly WPA-supported artists—the majority eventually filled the art departments of colleges or went into other employment—as America emerged from the Depression and the last years of the war brought an unprecedented economic boom. A mere 40 galleries existed in New York at the beginning of the war, mostly specializing in French painting. By 1946, there were 150 galleries, and much of the art they offered was domestically produced.

Institutional support for American art came hand-in-glove with corporate patronage and patriotic exhortations to "buy American." You had to buy American if you were going to buy anything, since the Second World War had curtailed the supply of available French painting. MoMA, Peggy Guggenheim's Art of This Century Gallery, and corporate buyers all engaged in nativist cultural boosterism during the war years; auction houses and private dealers, by 1944, were selling prodigious quantities of American art. Auction houses hit all-time record sales in 1945; "galleries reported a 37 percent increase in sales over the previous record year," Alice Goldfarb Marquis reports in *Art Czar: The Rise and Fall of Clement Greenberg*. "Average volume per gallery rose from 125 pictures to 160; prices were also higher, with about 20 percent of sales above $1,000."[1]

The American art being sold represented a narrow range of approaches to painting or sculpture: signature styles, though diverse, were all contained within defined boundaries that reflected a consensus of taste arrived at by what art historian Serge Guilbaut calls "the inner circle": Peggy Guggenheim, Alfred Barr, James Thrall Soby, James Johnson Sweeney, and Clement Greenberg.

Sweeney was the art critic for *Partisan Review* and also worked for Peggy Guggenheim; Barr was the founding director of MoMA; Soby and Sweeney both held important museum jobs while publishing art criticism; Greenberg had become the country's most powerful art critic after throwing down the gauntlet, in 1939, against popular culture in "Avant-Garde and Kitsch," a rather grim defense of "standards" published in *Partisan Review*.

Among other pronouncements, Greenberg had declared, "The masses have always remained more or less indifferent to culture in the process of development. But today such culture is being abandoned by those to whom it actually belongs—our ruling class." Our ruling class sat up and took notice of Greenberg's decree.

"Taste" had an ideological job to do, inseparable from the co-optation of "museum-quality" modernism into a cultural extension of the Cold War. American art needed a bold, innovative audacity to contrast with the drab, polemical realism advanced by the Soviet Union and its satellite nations. In contrast to a blatantly ideological, proletarian-populist Socialist Realism, American art would reflect the extreme outer boundaries of "artistic freedom" championed by its elitist inner circles—in Greenberg's words, its "ruling class." The quintessence of this unbridled freedom was located in the work of its most chaotic avatar: Jackson Pollock.

At the end of the 1940s, *Life* magazine featured an elaborate spread on new American artists that included photos of Jackson Pollock frenetically splashing paint on canvases on his studio floor. Was he, the magazine rhetorically asked, "the greatest living painter in America?" While it's been argued that *Life* obviously didn't think so and offered Pollock and other abstract artists up for ridicule, Henry Luce's *Time-Life-Fortune* media empire had an unfailing grasp of the prime tenet of public relations: ink is ink. Alfred Barr had convinced Luce that nothing reflected America's unique democratic freedom better than these wild and crazy abstract artists the cognoscenti were going ape over.

Millions who would never have heard of Pollock otherwise (in 1949 *Life*'s circulation was roughly 5.3 million) were drawn into excited arguments over Action Painting, Abstract Expressionism, and the New York School—essentially different names for the same roster of artworks and artists. From Pollock's new celebrity followed the ascendancy of other careers and reputations, based on art that, in one way or another, embodied a consistent image that the institutional arbiters of American art wanted to disseminate.

Many alleged innovations of the new American art—biomorphic forms, symbolically titled abstractions, bizarre juxtapositions of imaginary objects, mythically evocative, nonrealist tableaux—were adapted, dissembled, or grabbed outright from the work of wartime Surrealist exiles. But the homemade American product arrived Handi-Wrapped in star-spangled clichés of cowboy individualism, the churning inner torment of the artist to "express" himself (it was all but exclusively "him"), and alcohol-ravaged, self-immolating struggles to achieve pure painting as its own raison d'être, painting without reference to a world beyond the canvas.

Despite the non-objective and hermetic bent of "the New Painting"—whether one called it Action Painting, Abstract Expressionism, or an exemplar of the New York School (to simplify matters, these terms can be collapsed into Abstract Expressionism, or simply "the New Art")—its inherent notions of heroicism, of evoking spiritual vastness, of wrestling with the ineffable and taming it into iconography, had deep roots in the eulogistic Noble Savagery and primal wilderness themes of sublimity found in earlier American painters like Thomas Cole, Frederick Church, and Homer Dodge Martin; it shared something of the same provincialism and the same conflation of white male heterosexual subjectivity with "universal" values and emotions.

The canvas was the arena of inner struggle made palpable, the archaeology of its own protean creation. The combative romanticism of Jackson Pollock, the garrulous self-involvement of Barnett Newman, the misogynist brio of Willem de Kooning, and the bipolar quest for the Absolute of Mark Rothko, among other pathologies enacted on canvas (every artist, in every medium, inscribes his or her pathology in the work of art), received inexhaustible, authoritative cheerleading from powerful critics like Greenberg and Harold Rosenberg, former Trotskyites who had ditched the idea that art should have any social or political content.

The inner torment of the Abstract Expressionists, according to their supporters, resulted in visual graphs of anxiety that mirrored the collective unconscious. These artists excavated the very bowels of the human soul; their art sprang from the same timeless archetypes and symbols found in aboriginal carvings, cave paintings, and other residua of prehistoric hunter-gatherers, a notion squeezed from Jungian psychology like lemon juice and one that implicitly defined artmaking as a male activity. Particularly in the work of de Kooning, the canvas played the role of the passive female surface to the virile manipulations of the male painter.

It's startling today to realize how much power art critics exercised in the heyday of Greenberg and

Rosenberg. They had little detailed knowledge of art history, but knew important art when they saw it. The two critics became mortal enemies after a brief friendship; though they were advocates for the same artists, each could prove that the other liked the same thing for the wrong reasons. They trafficked in the jargon of "greatness," of "major" and "minor," "important," "groundbreaking," and so on, the broad-brush vocabulary of subjective opinion marshaling a quorum. This language of consensus-building, of gathering a claque around a proper name, carried weight at a time when few Americans were familiar with any sort of art, and the sheer assertiveness of these critics attracted attention for the New Art in larger media venues than the small magazines that published their writings.

But for all of the publicity surrounding Abstract Expressionism, the public reaction to it was overwhelmingly negative. The hype, in the short run, did little for the sales and income of the artists, who remained a hard sell. Instead, over time, it enriched the small, elite group of collectors whose purchases were gradually ratified by institutional acquisition of the same artists. "Buy low, sell high" is the enduring principle of the art world as well as the stock market. In time, the artists too would materially benefit, but then, as now, they pushed the caboose on the gravy train.

Although the New Art initially garnered more publicity than actual sales, what Greenberg and the Abstract Expressionists devised, avant la lettre, was the phenomenon of "personal branding": the assertion of individualism by marketing a distinctively packaged brand of the same product, brought to you by a distinct and vivid personality. It was this, rather than a preoccupation with what the artist had "inside," that would carry over into Pop Art and all the art movements that followed after it.

The artists themselves didn't necessarily view themselves as members of any movement or school; each had his or her quiddities and ideas, individual techniques, formal goals. Many thought Greenberg ridiculous, Rosenberg overly florid, and both critics deleterious presences in the art world, yet their support was crucial to an artist's inclusion in a congealing historical canon.

The Abstract Expressionist painters were violently antipathetic toward younger artists doing different kinds of work. Proto-Pop foreigners like Arman and Eduardo Paolozzi, domestic anomalies like Wallace Berman and Peter Blake, crypto-realists like Richard Lindner, Ray Johnson, Peter Blake, and Ed Kienholz, were beyond the pale of acceptability, while such older figurative painters as Philip Evergood, Robert Vickrey,

George Tooker, Jack Levine, Alton Pickens, and Paul Cadmus were considered leftovers from another era.

By 1949, the Abstract Expressionists had coalesced into a men's club, headquartered at the Cedar Bar, which disparaged all but a handful of female artists, expressed real hatred of homosexuals, bathed in a sea of booze every night, and considered the only place for blacks in the arts a jazz club. What had become, in effect, "the New York art world" was an utterly unwelcoming environment for a figure like Andy Warhol, who prudently put his "high art" ambitions on hold, immersed himself in commercial art, and waited with steel-willed patience for his moment to arrive.

TWO

Warhol moved to New York with fellow Carnegie graduate Philip Pearlstein in 1949—just in time for one of the weirdest decades America had ever known. Postwar America was marked by two contradictory preoccupations. Technical advances and financial opportunities seemed limitless, from the Salk polio vaccine to affordable home appliances, from easy mortgages in garden suburbs to reasonably priced cars. At the same time, from the first successful Soviet atomic test in 1949

emerged the very real threat that all life could be vapor-
ized into random particles in minutes or disastrously
mutated into bizarre forms by atomic radiation.

Atomic Armageddon quickly became the metaphor-
ical fodder for hundreds of B movies—*Godzilla*, *The
Day the Earth Stood Still*, *The Blob*, *It Came from Outer
Space*, *These Are the Damned*, *Tarantula*, *The Incredible
Shrinking Man*, *Attack of the Fifty-Foot Woman*, *The
Thing*, and *When Worlds Collide*, to name a few. (When
the cultural wheel finally turned and perpetual menace
reached its inevitable saturation point, apocalypse met
its slapstick match in Terry Southern's script for Stanley
Kubrick's *Dr. Strangelove, or How I Stopped Worrying
and Learned to Love the Bomb*.)

Television provided nightly seizures of constipating
terror with thermonuclear disaster narratives in pro-
grams like *The Outer Limits*, *Way Out*, and *The Twi-
light Zone*. Typically, a prudent, wholesome family
constructed a basement bomb shelter stocked with am-
ple food, water purification tablets, and air filtration
systems (throughout the fifties, American families received fat manila envelopes from Civil Defense stuffed
with life-saving goodies in military drab-olive cans and
phials), while profligate neighbors, caught mid-martini
by an onslaught of incoming ICBMs, attacked the forti-
fied bunker next door with lawn mowers, chainsaws,

crowbars, and whatever else they could find in the garage, endangering the survival of all.

Another fear that suffused this era of unparalleled economic boom was the possibility that Americans were becoming too much alike, ossified into unrewarding conformity. The consumer Nirvana that followed World War II had created a standardized version of "the good life" at conspicuous odds with the country's mythos of rugged individualism. Suburban uniformity and the fear of standing out in the crowd perplexed sociologists and pop psychologists in books such as Sloan Wilson's *The Man in the Gray Flannel Suit*, Vance Packard's *The Hidden Persuaders*, Philip Wylie's *A Generation of Vipers*, J. K. Galbraith's *The Affluent Society*, David Reisman's *The Lonely Crowd*, and William H. Whyte's *The Organization Man*.

Films dramatized the fear of being "taken over" by emotional blankness and sinister cerebral clarity, promoting unease about "being like everybody else." Jack Finney's *Invasion of the Body Snatchers* was the most succinct articulation of the country's nascent anxiety about homogenization. Interplanetary pods begin "replacing" humans, when they fall asleep, with emotionless replicas who carry on the everyday lives of their victims, but without the bothersome differences in temperament and ideas that make for a diverse and difficult world. The pod people can exist free of grief, romantic love, disappointment, joy, and everything else that might be associated with "soul": Finney's dystopian fantasia had myriad offshoots in films and fictions about "cold" scientists who viewed a zombielike unanimity as the solution to all human conflict. "Imagine a world without pain, without feeling," was a standard mad scientist's enticement in this kind of movie to recalcitrant individualists who resisted being replaced by communitarian duplicates. Finney minted the perfect metaphor for communism *and* consumerist uniformity.

Apart from science fiction movies specializing in emotional erasure themes, Huston's *The Asphalt Jungle*, Ray's *Rebel Without a Cause*, and virtually any film by Douglas Sirk dramatized the period's social, political, and sexual asphyxia, while the Doris Day–Rock Hudson–Tony Randall school of chaste sex comedies pandered to the allure of transgression while squashing it, resolving suspected infidelities, flirtations, criminal intentions, and so on, into celebrations of the sublimated sadomasochism of the ad agency, the wisdom of the patriarchal family, the wholesome ignorance of carnal relations even among married Americans with children.

Andy Warhol eventually adopted the blankness and lack of feeling feared by many Americans who felt "taken over" by the consumer lifestyle. This gradual makeover followed years of eager-to-please, obsequious hustling in the world of magazine and fashion illustration, which catered precisely to consumerism and sharpened Warhol's sense that what people wanted and what people feared were simply facets of the same insecurity.

THREE

A ndy Warhol flourished in his early career in advertising. He was a favorite of magazine editors, for whom he always produced an array of illustrations to choose from, delivered in paper bags—"Andy Paperbag" was his bedraggled persona of the period.

Warhol showed his work in galleries as early as 1952, when the Hugo Gallery exhibited his illustrations of Truman Capote's writings. In 1954 he had two shows at the Loft Gallery on Forty-fifth Street, the first an array of folded-paper sculptures arranged on the floor, the other drawings of dancer John Butler.

But the principal showcase for Warhol's work during this phase was a fashionable ice cream parlor and notions store, the Serendipity Café, owned by friends of Warhol's who helped furnish his first apartment. These little exhibitions were worlds away from "the art world" that Warhol wanted into, the rarefied realm of art dealers like Sidney Janis, Betty Parsons, Tibor de Nagy, and Martha Jackson and artists like Barnett Newman, Willem de Kooning, and Robert Motherwell; the serious art of the day was heavy, portentous, and generally humorless, a thick imbroglio of polemics and agonic practices that an artist like Warhol, having nothing to offer, could only gaze at with somewhat baffled envy.

Warhol's aesthetic sensibilities were unusually frank and unfiltered in his noncommercial drawings and paintings of the 1950s, and this "serious" work kept him at the margins of the "high art" realm, not only because of its obdurately representational bent, but because it depicted, or alluded to, homoeroticism and shared with Warhol's commercial art certain twee and whimsical qualities redolent of homosexuality and the form of delectation known as "camp."

The rarefied stylization of commercial illustration in the 1950s, its "effeminate" delicacy and decorative excess, exuberance of detail and often fetishistic treatment of its subject matter, was by no means controversial, but normative: commercial art was one field where being, or seeming, gay carried no particular stigma and posed no discernible threat to the status quo. Fashion illustration, particularly, was geared to a female clientele; its theatrical ornamentation and jewel-like preciosity were exactly the features most appealing to consumers of the products being advertised, and the editors who commissioned this kind of art were unfazed by the presumed sexual orientation of the artists they hired. Illustration was a safe haven for homosexuals, who, in the 1950s, were pointedly unwelcome in more "serious" professions, including that of the "serious" artist.

The anticommunist hysteria of the 1950s was intricately linked to social taboos of many kinds. The fear-mongering purveyed by aggressive anticommunism further played upon other societal fears as part of its agenda—the early manifestations of the black civil rights movement were attributed to "Communist agitation," and the virtually unspeakable realm of homosexuality was often, speakably, linked to "Communist subversion"—homosexuality was widely regarded as a mental disease, a threat to the normative nuclear family, and, in the realms of government, a secret malady whose sufferers were vulnerable to blackmail and the surrender of state secrets to the nation's enemies.

On the artistic front, the U.S. State Department was actively engaged in promoting American art, especially Abstract Expressionism, as evidence of American "free expression"—in reality, a type of artistic expression with no polemical axes to grind and no political agendas; moreover, its avatars, aside from a few token females, were "real men," two-fisted paint-slingers like Jackson Pollock, to whom any taint of sexual nonconformity was anathema. This dominant fine art establishment, which only began to develop cracks in the middle and late 1950s, had no vectors of entrée for an artist like Andy Warhol. Ironically or not, the two artists whose works most effectively broke up the hegemony of Abstract Expressionism, Jasper Johns and Robert Rauschenberg, were both gay—but so discreetly gay that their art effectively concealed it, and they shared a disdain for artists like Warhol who exhibited "gay" mannerisms or produced work with any marked homoerotic proclivities.

Until Warhol commenced his bid for "fine art" attention, Andy the Dandy, Andy Paperbag, Raggedy Andy worked in a field where his homosexuality was undoubtedly assumed and posed no threat to his employment prospects. Andy Warhola, whose last name, legendarily, was accidentally abbreviated in a magazine credit and stayed that way (a nice story, but he'd often dropped the "a" at the end of his name in college), could assume the honorary, protective coloration of one of "nature's bachelors," as homosexuals were sometimes slyly referred to at the time. At the tail end of the 1950s, Warhol recognized a paradigm shift in the world of "high art" and started pushing in earnest, with every workaholic sinew, to find his way into it. His efforts got no initial support from Johns and Rauschenberg.

In 1958, Emile de Antonio, a filmmaker who also acted as a kind of artists' agent, was brutally frank when Warhol asked him why Rauschenberg and Johns didn't like him: they thought he was "too swish," and somewhat inexplicably, they faulted him for collecting works by other artists (including a drawing by Johns)— a practice with long historical precedents, though according to them, it just wasn't done. (At the time, Warhol's little collection included small works by Braque, Magritte, Miró, and Klee.) Rauschenberg and Johns decorated windows for Bonwit's, just as Andy did. Using a made-up, composite name, "Matson Jones," *they* dressed windows to survive, but Andy was *famous* for it. And so on.

At least one critic has suggested that Warhol's "collecting," for Johns and Rauschenberg, marked Warhol as a *consumer* rather than a *producer*, and that "consumption," in this context, was connected to the "feminine" activity of shopping. (Perhaps this was true, though Warhol's peers-to-be couldn't possibly have envisioned the fantastic scope and promiscuity of Warhol's "collecting," which included every conceivable kind of collectable object, from cookie jars to gemstones, in a hoard of jaw-dropping magnitude that filled Warhol's successive townhouses and, after his death, would result in a ten-day-long auction at Christie's.) But certainly they were more directly alarmed by Andy's flaunting of gay mannerisms. In the '50s, a flaming queen in the room was a psychological threat to any closeted gays in his vicinity, as if their own "unmanly" traits might be betrayed by sheer proximity.

FOUR

While modern art was lampooned in the tabloids, detested by most of the public that took any notice of it, and greeted with trite epithets of charlatanism and fraud by traditionalist artists and educators, its most clamorous enemies in the late 1940s and early '50s could be found among the Great Apes of the United States Congress, who were eager to capitalize on Senator Joseph McCarthy's crusade against domestic subversion wherever it could be imagined to exist. During their European honeymoon, McCarthy's aides Roy Cohn and David Schine even cleansed U.S. Information Agency (USIA) and armed forces libraries abroad of books containing un-American themes and stories. Some thirty thousand all told, the list included books by Jean-Paul Sartre, Alberto Moravia, Sherwood Anderson, Pearl S. Buck, Erskine Caldwell, John Dewey, John Dos Passos, Upton Sinclair, Dashiell Hammett, Howard Fast, Arthur Miller, Mickey Spillane, Edgar Snow, Norman Mailer, Georges Simenon, Langston Hughes, Ernest Hemingway, and Theodore Dreiser. Also expunged from U.S.-sponsored cultural events abroad were works of composers such as Aaron Copland and exhibitions of architects such as Frank Lloyd Wright.

The political crusade against modernist painting was triggered by a State Department plan that began in the late 1940s: to send "advanced" American art abroad in a series of government-sponsored exhibitions as part of a wide-reaching propaganda effort on behalf of "the American way of life."

Not everyone saw a flowering of free expression in modernism, and many intent on bringing free expression to "enslaved" countries didn't much believe in allowing free expression in America. A Missouri congressman named George Dondero led a charge by legislators by declaring that "all modern art is Communistic," citing the specific wiles and devious methods by which Cubism, Futurism, Dada, "Expressionism," and "Abstractionism" sought to demoralize and mentally unbalance Americans and ultimately—tools of the Kremlin that these artists all were—destroy Americanism, an increasingly ill-defined and ever-diminishing quality, or quantity.

A lunatic, obviously. Like many lunatics, Dondero enjoyed enthusiastic support from other lunatics. One of Dondero's posse revealed that "modern art is actually a means of espionage . . . if you know how to read them, modern paintings will disclose the weak spots in U.S. fortifications, and such crucial structures as Boulder Dam."[2] This must have come as startling news to artists who had little familiarity with Boulder Dam and other crucial structures or fortifications. The idea of Communist spies meticulously scanning reproductions of Pollock's *Blue Poles* with magnifying glasses and decoder rings really was McCarthyism in a nutshell. Whether or not the artist carried some memory of this legislator's paranoid fantasy in mind, one of Warhol's last paintings, a crude black-and-white map indicating known Soviet missile sites, carries a rich irony indeed. (A further irony: Warhol's father had worked on the construction of Boulder Dam.)

Dondero and company caused endless trouble for the State Department, which endorsed Eisenhower's strategically liberal view of modernist art. The artist should be free to realize his or her autonomous vision without state interference. "As long as artists are at liberty to feel with high personal intensity, as long as our artists are free to create with sincerity and conviction, there will be a healthy controversy and progress in art," Eisenhower declared in an address on freedom in the arts in 1954. "How different it is in a tyranny. When artists are made the slaves and tools of the state; when artists become chief propagandists of a cause, progress is arrested and creation and genius are destroyed."[3] Socialist Realism, the approved art of the Communist world, restricted the artist to oversaturated realist paintings of joyful workers driving tractors and their beaming comrades operating industrial machinery. (Of course, such works were not terribly different from the kind of thing most Americans recognized as art, most typically in the form of Norman Rockwell's cover paintings for the *Saturday Evening Post.*)

The more shrouded enclaves of American government also embraced the clear propaganda value of showing the new art abroad. As they habitually did and still do, they resorted to covert means of achieving their goal rather than attempting to seek funding through legislation. The CIA, using agent Tom Braden as its point man, laundered the money for overseas exhibitions through a network of private foundations and institutions (primarily the Museum of Modern Art). Known as the Planning Coordination Group and presided over by Nelson Rockefeller, this company "oversaw all National Security Council decisions, including CIA covert operations."[4] The Rockefeller brothers' bank, Chase Manhattan, was among the first to decorate its interiors with abstract paintings.

Numerous MoMA trustees had close ties to the company. Jock Whitney had belonged to the CIA's forerunner, the OSS (Office of Strategic Services), and after the war he established J. H. Whitney & Company, "a partnership dedicated to the propagation of the free-enterprise system."

One partner in Whitney's venture, William H. Jackson, was the CIA's deputy director. William Burden, appointed chairman of MoMA's advisory committee in 1940, had been president of the CIA's Fairfield Foundation.

It would take an entire chapter to cite the names and résumés of MoMA trustees, consultants, committee chairmen, and others employed by the museum while engaged in propaganda and intelligence work for the CIA and clandestine funding of anticommunist left publications such as *Encounter*.

Questions inevitably arise when "unpolitical art" is used for political ends, or when the success or failure of artists depends on their complicity with propaganda. Many Abstract Expressionists and other artists chosen for deluxe exposure in lavish foreign exhibitions during the 1950s had been intensely involved in the politics of the 1930s, whether as Communists, fellow-travelers, Trotskyites, Stalinists, socialists, or anticommunist leftists. It's improbable that none of them suspected the purpose for which they were being used; it is also revealing that nobody rejected the blandishments of celebrity, however questionable its vectors.

Personal success trumped political conviction, probably for many reasons. Unlike artists in the Communist world, American artists weren't being asked to inject any state-dictated content into what they were doing or to introduce ideology into their paintings—which, in the case of Abstract Expressionism, would hardly have been possible anyway. Artists want their work to be seen and shown as widely as possible, a perfectly natural desire. Moreover, one of Abstract Expressionism's goals was to raise American art from its provincial status to parity with, if not dominance over, its European "betters."

In effect, the agenda of the State Department was no different than the agendas of the artists themselves; if they understood that they were being used to "fight communism" on the cultural front, the battleground wasn't in Russia or its satellite states, but in Western Europe, the art of which had long been held up as superior to anything produced by Americans.

FIVE

During the glory years of Abstract Expressionism, Warhol had something of a love-hate relationship with the work promoted in the art world. It was not the kind of art he wanted to do; he was impressed and intimidated by it, and probably repulsed by the personalities of its premier practitioners, whose homophobia was as legendary as their boozing.

While it was obscured during Warhol's lifetime by his Pop Art career, his commercial artwork during the 1950s has by now been extensively documented, both in the biographies written about him and in the many lavishly illustrated books devoted to his work.

Trained at Carnegie Tech to be a good commercial-art professional, Warhol quickly achieved success as a graphic illustrator and within a few years of his arrival in New York had become one of the best-known and most highly paid commercial artists, sought after by magazines like *Glamour*, *Harper's Bazaar*, *Vogue*, *McCall's*, and *Vanity Fair* and by ad agencies such as Young & Rubican. While other commercial artists of the era made their work as "photographic-looking" as possible, Warhol developed a distinctive, hand-drawn look in his ad work that was instantly recognizable. He produced advertising drawings for products like Martini & Rossi wines and Fleming Joffe leathers. His distinctive line drawings as well as his blotted-line style of easily reproducible imagery adorned book jackets for New Directions and covers for jazz albums by Kenny Burrell and Count Basie; undoubtedly his best-known advertising work was done for I. Miller Shoes, the premier shoe emporium of its day whose ads appeared weekly between 1955 and 1957 in the *Sunday New York Times* in the section devoted to wedding announcements.

He won four awards from the Art Directors Club in the 1950s, three of them for his shoe drawings for I. Miller advertisements. Indeed, Warhol's headiest success as an illustrator was in his endlessly inventive, often boldly exaggerated designs of ladies' shoes. But much of his other graphic work gleaned wide exposure—for example, a drawing of a sailor injecting his arm with heroin in an ad for a radio crime program on "The Nation's Nightmare" that occupied a full page of the *New York Times* in September 1951, then became the cover of an album of the radio program. This won Warhol his first Art Directors Club gold medal in 1953.

Warhol's "fine art" efforts throughout the 1950s reflect two alternating, sometimes jarringly combined, distinct tendencies. Many of these pieces used virtually the same stippled, blotted, or continuous-line techniques of his commercial works, while others incorporated an emphatic painterly drizzle and motes of scumbled brushwork imitative of Abstract Expressionism. He produced thousands of "private drawings" and collages and a smaller number of paintings, many now lost or destroyed; between 1952 and 1959, he collaborated with various "boyfriends" and others on privately printed books—*A Is an Alphabet*, *25 Cats Named Sam and One Blue Pussy*, *A La Recherche du Shoe Perdu*, *In the Bottom of My Garden*, *Wild Raspberries*—whose contents were usually exhibited at the Bodley Gallery on East Sixtieth Street. The books themselves were typically presented as gifts to art directors and other of Warhol's commercial clients and featured Julia Warhola's distinctive, uneven handwriting, knotted with spelling errors, which Andy also employed for some of his advertising work.

A vast quantity of noncommercial Warhol art from the 1950s has come to light in recent years. Much of it has been no more precisely dated yet than "1950s," and it is difficult, if not impossible, to chart any salient "development," beyond its obvious skill and cleverness, before Warhol "began Pop Art." It includes fanciful and rococo colored drawings of cupids, butterflies, flowers, pastries, and animals; portraiture and depictions of male bodies executed in ballpoint pen in a manner reminiscent of Cocteau, as if rendered without lifting the pen from the page; feet and shoes, male nudes, and everyday objects like paintbrushes, putty knives, gloves, hats, tubes of lipstick, and the like; in 1956 and 1957 particularly, Warhol employed imitation gold and silver leaf for the surfaces of myriad ink drawings—of monkeys, peacocks, horses, angels, floral bouquets, male profiles, body parts, and, most notably, shoes.

In a show at the Bodley Gallery in 1956, Warhol exhibited numerous collage-drawings of shoes incorporating gold and silver foil, each of which was given the name of a famous personality (Mae West, Julie Andrews, Kate Smith, Truman Capote, James Dean). These "golden slippers" were reproduced in *Life* magazine's "Speaking of Pictures" section in a two-page spread in its January 1957 issue. Although the "celebrity shoes" were briefly reviewed by Parker Tyler in *Art News*, *Life* featured them in its section devoted to visual oddities rather than fine art. Throughout the 1950s, Warhol's shows in such marginal venues as the Serendipity Café and the Bodley Gallery were given perfunctory attention, when noted at all, in the art press.

Broadly speaking, Warhol's noncommercial art of the 1950s was redolent of both the strictly representational nature of his commercial design work and his preoccupation with the frivolous motifs and blatantly homoerotic content that "marked" him as an outsider to the art establishment. And when Warhol sensed, in the final years of the 1950s, that the burgeoning phenomenon of Pop Art could provide his entrée into a nascent "movement" that was nudging aside Abstract Expressionism as the fine art du jour, he intuitively abandoned the overtly homosexual features of his earlier work, as well as the upper-middle-class subject matter of his commissioned graphic design art, from which he had extrapolated so much of his noncommercial art.

Even an infinite number of elegant shoe illustrations and fey exhibitions of figurative drawings would never kick down the door to the realm of "fine art"; it would take something else entirely to do that. Warhol perceived, in the transitional art of Jasper Johns, Robert Rauschenberg, and Larry Rivers, an opening into that realm. When early Pop Art began creeping into the inventories of high-end galleries like Castelli, Warhol understood how his years of doing commercial art could serve his larger ambitions.

SIX

In the summer of 1952, Julia Warhola moved into Andy's basement apartment on East Seventy-fifth

Street. She arrived with her bags to look after "her Andy." They slept in the same bedroom. They acquired two Siamese cats. These became many Siamese cats. Despite impossible clutter and Andy's lack of work space, mother and son seemed to enjoy each other's company.

In 1953 they moved to a larger apartment on Lexington Avenue in the twenties, shared for a time with an art director friend, Leonard Kessler. Julia and Andy again shared a bedroom. The ever-growing cat population exuded a dizzying stench, while the noise from Shirley's Pin-Up Bar on the ground floor blasted through the windows.

In the townhouses he later acquired, Julia's living space was confined to the basements, where she carried on, it was said, a completely hermetic life in the middle of Manhattan, inhabited by memories of her Ruthenian girlhood, alienated from the outer world, and venturing outside only to go to church. She began drinking Scotch throughout the day.

Julia returned to Pittsburgh once, angered that Andy's financial help to the rest of the family was less generous than he could afford. Warhol couldn't manage without her. He soon invited her back. Art director Joseph Giordano, whom Julia demanded be present when she returned, later recalled the scene: "She slammed her suitcases on the floor, looked at [Andy], and said 'I'm Andy Warhol.' And there was a big discussion about why she was Andy Warhol . . . the crux of Andy Warhol is that he felt so unloved, so unloved. I know it came from his mother. . . . She made him feel insignificant. She made him feel that he was the ugliest creature God ever put on this earth."[5]

Over the twenty years that Andy and Julia lived together in Manhattan, their relationship was a mixture of mutual support and antagonism. They seem to have kept one another amused and infuriated. Julia could never entirely control Andy, but Andy easily controlled her. True, her presence kept him leashed to a suffocation he wanted to escape; yet it provided a stability and nourishment he apparently needed.

Whatever antagonisms rankled between Warhol and Julia, she took care of his basic needs, serenely infantilized him, kept him safe from adult development. Her presence turned his homes into closets. Whenever she met one of Andy's female "Superstars," Julia urged her to marry him.

In his characteristically insightful essay "Queer Andy," critic and activist Simon Watney perfectly captures the Freudian dynamics of Andy Warhol's childhood and its persistence in the contradictory, controlling behavior of the adult artist. "He seems to have lived with his mother in Manhattan to guarantee the undermining of any sexual self-confidence he might have achieved, just as throughout his adult life he played his immediate friends and colleagues against one another as he had learned to play members of his family against one another when he was a child."[6]

The neurotic re-creation in adult life of familial dysfunction and its participants is an insidious imperative of the unconscious. The family is both the cauldron of insanity and the site of physical safety and nourishment. The reprise of an original family configuration in adulthood, however, produces a corrosive, womblike pathology and a chimerical kind of security. Seeking friends who correspond to the figures of our childhood, we gravitate to the flaws, addictions, destructive patterns, and emotional disorders we learned to consider intrinsic to our comfort zones rather than the strengths and virtues that offset their negative impact.

Warhol's eventual arena of family reenactment, the Factory, became one of the most significant cultural phenomena of its time. The adult Warhol was an anomaly in this re-creation: a figure, commanding massive cultural space, whose most evident feature was a massive lack.

His mother purportedly advised him not to be pushy but to let everybody know he was around. Andy, it seems, found a way to be pushy without being overtly aggressive: by simply withholding attention from people who displeased him. He manufactured a space too large for himself that could not be satisfyingly filled by others; it could only be controlled by the punitive exercise of his will.

SEVEN

Warhol is said to have had many sexual affairs, despite Julia's presence in his apartments. He went home with other people. One anonymous informant told Bockris that Warhol was skilled and uninhibited in bed.

Unrequited infatuations, obsessions with unavailable men, and friendships Andy vainly hoped would flower into "relationships" are amply documented. Romanticism permeated his delicate, often fey and fetishistic drawings of the 1950s: whimsical fairy tale creatures people his privately produced books of drawings.

Warhol had an early obsession with Truman Capote. He was in love, if not with Capote, then with what Capote represented: androgynous prettiness, social connections, money, and fame. Warhol's Capote fixation became onerous to the writer. Andy had managed a brief, bar-crawling relationship with Capote's mother,

Nina, but Capote decided that Warhol was pathetic and quickly cut him off.

An earlier crush on television set designer Charles Lisanby resulted in a shared trip across several Asian countries. After a queasy start, attributed to Warhol's unwelcome overtures and jealous rages, the adventure unfolded amiably. Warhol's drawings of their travels are fascinating little masterpieces of ruins, temples, street life, masques, and costumes. Yet upon their return to New York, Warhol stalked off by himself at the airport. He bitterly told friends that he had "gone around the world with a boy and never got a kiss."

Warhol had a talent for holding grudges. It's doubtful that Lisanby wouldn't have known the nature of Warhol's interest in him. Perhaps he wasn't attracted to Warhol but obtained something from Warhol's company that he deliberately misrepresented as the possibility of an affair. Perhaps Lisanby believed he could acquire something of Warhol's abilities while holding out the promise of an eventual sexual liaison.

EIGHT

A yearning side of Warhol's personality seems incompatible with his famously detached persona.

But he expressed it often enough, in scornfully unemotive terms. He wished, throughout college at Carnegie Tech and later with a succession of flatmates in New York, to "share problems." His often quoted remarks that having feelings is too hard and too painful, the cold aphorisms he coined as armor against emotional hurt—these comments simultaneously reveal and repress Warhol's obvious vulnerability.

"I want to be a machine," he once said. Trying to be a machine is hard work, however easier it makes perceiving others as utilitarian objects. To be unloved and to wish for love truly is "too hard"—unless one reverts to an almost impossible stoicism.

Warhol's stifling of emotional display can be seen in his self-makeover in the early '60s, when the eager-to-please, dandyish "Raggedy Andy" of the commercial art world began to invade posh parties with entourages of marauding underground types, having adopted a tougher, invulnerable carapace: leather jackets, jeans, ungovernably messy wigs (he was going prematurely bald), sunglasses, Teddy Boy ankle boots. The pathological shyness of his childhood was transformed into a menacing aversion to being touched, a glazed and distant unapproachability.

Warhol's reinvention of himself as a brittle, silent, withholding specter emphasized his reversed position vis-à-vis the imperious, demanding fashion editors and graphic designers he'd catered to throughout the 1950s. He would no longer play the desiring half of any unreturned attention.

Within this persona, there was also an aggressively passive response to the "AbEx" crew. Warhol made no effort to emulate the male artists of that movement or to fit in with either their aesthetic or their macho exploits. He began "playing up" the effeminacy, the challenging silence behind the shyness, the air of autistic indifference to what other people thought about him. This was a bravura refusal to appear in any way vulnerable, either to the withering ridicule of established heterosexual artists or to his own inability to connect with other people emotionally, to his longing for "real" relationships, or to the intense pain caused by his sense of inferiority, instilled by his mother and exacerbated by his later rejection by men he desired.

As Warhol puts it in *POPism: The Warhol Sixties*:

So I decided I just wasn't going to care, because those were all things I didn't want to change anyway, that I didn't think I should want to change. There was nothing wrong with being a commercial artist and there was nothing wrong with collecting art that you admired. . . . And as for the "swish" thing, I'd always had a lot of fun with that. . . . You'd have to have seen the way all the Abstract Expressionists carried themselves . . . to understand how shocked people were to see a painter coming on swish. I certainly wasn't a butch kind of guy by nature, but I must admit, I went out of my way to play up the other extreme.[7]

This brittle, distancing attitude dominated the studio atmosphere as well; all that mattered was the steady production of work, regardless of whatever cacophony (loud music, blaring television sets, the amphetamine-fueled antics of people hanging around and rushing in and out) ruled the day. At his studios—his second homes—Warhol was the presiding spirit, the unquestioned boss. He seldom said anything. Others knew, almost telepathically, how he wanted things. No one was ever invited into Andy's houses after he became famous. Relatives from Pittsburgh were welcome to visit on weekends. He got on best with children.

The exclusion of friends from his living spaces was an incremental process and another chapter in his evolving legend. People might imagine all sorts of secret things going on inside his homes. Andy never divulged what he did or, more likely, didn't do in private. In this way he could at least pretend to have a "private life." Ultimately, even the pretense of having one became unnecessary.

It may be a cliché that the longer a person wears a mask, the more it becomes his true face. But the cliché is often true.

NINE

Warhol conceived Pop Art as the negation of subjectivity: the refusal of sentiment, sadness, disappointment. Just as Warhol excised, to all appearances, these qualities from his own personality, the Warhol work ethic became as hard as the steel that rolled from Pittsburgh's factories. Similarly, the "factory" ethic informed his work and life. Perhaps this ethic was born on the streets of Pittsburgh, or even at Carnegie Tech. It is well known that Andrew Carnegie built the institution to resemble a factory, often remarking that if it failed in its educational mission it would be easy enough to repurpose the buildings for manufacturing.

The transition from Warhol's fey, delicate, expressively hand-drawn art of the '50s to Pop Art entailed a brusque repudiation of the "personal" in the content, although Warhol vacillated, in many paintings from 1960, between a glacially hard-edged approach to his new subject matter and the inclusion of the drips, spatters, scumbled areas of paint, and tentative lines associated with the "high art" recognized in the 1950s. His fledgling Pop works frequently exist in two versions. His metamorphosis began with primarily black-and-white paintings of the kinds of product advertisements found in tabloid newspapers and with the iconography of comic strip panels; Warhol's ambivalence about technique is baldly evident in double versions of works like *Storm Door* (1960). In one picture the stark lines and strict geometric picturing of a $12.99 storm door have been "softened" or blunted by arbitrary dribbles of black polymer paint, a nebulous area of smudgy gray brush strokes in the upper area of the picture, and the nervously tapered, inexact lines of the storm door itself; the other version reproduces the precise graphics of the advertisement, excluding all "evidence of the hand."

The same hesitance to forgo some "artistic" touches in favor of a more audacious, straightforward reproduction of his source material turns up in most of Warhol's black-and-white paintings derived from ads, in the form of rough drawing marks, splotches of paint, and drips; likewise, in Warhol's comic strip paintings, such as *Superman* (1960), *Dick Tracy* (1960), and *Nancy* (1960), blotches of underpainting, faint colored lines

extraneous to the image, and dialogue balloons partially obscured by washes of white paint appear.

By mid-1960, however, Warhol had decisively abandoned—either on advice from Ivan Karp or Emile de
Antonio or on his own, depending on whose version you
read—any gratuitously "painterly" mannerisms from
his work. Victor Bockris's remarkable biography, *The
Life and Death of Andy Warhol*, quotes de Antonio
thus: "[Andy] had painted two pictures of Coke bottles
about six feet tall. One was just a pristine black-and-
white Coke bottle. The other had a lot of abstract expressionist marks on it. I said, 'Come on, Andy, the
abstract one is a piece of shit, the other one is remarkable. It's our society, it's who we are, it's absolutely
beautiful and naked, and you ought to destroy the first
one and show the other.'"[8]

chapter three

POP ART: SURF'S UP!

ONE

ROM ABOUT 1955 ON, THE CRITICAL SUPPORT STRUC-
tures of the New York School became increasingly irrelevant to what was going on. Even
Abstract Expressionism's champions conceded that its
thematic concerns, if not its technical strategies, had
had their day. Fluxus, Funk Art, "happenings," per-
formance art, hybrid combinations of painting, sculpture, body art, music, dance, so-called underground film
and theater, were steadily emerging among the
cognoscenti as playful yet powerful alternatives to the
staunch seriousness of the art being featured in upscale

galleries and acquired by museums. These new, outrageous forms of expression erased rigid boundaries between popular and elitist art. The influence of rock and roll, African American blues and jazz, and electronic music had a direct impact on the other arts: if you were listening to Robert Johnson or John Coltrane or Elvis Presley, or Stockhausen or Lucio Berio, what "higher" pleasure did a Barnett Newman zip painting give you? Inevitably, the meshing of "high" and "low" aesthetic expression prevailing in the alternative art scene found champions in new critics; establishment galleries scrambled to acquire these new kinds of art; and collectors followed suit.

To understand the shock that Andy Warhol and Pop Art inflicted on AbEx, one need only look to the pyramid structure that had been imposed on the fine art world. The rationale for a hierarchy of aesthetic pleasures was that some art was ennobling and other art coarsening. The designation of sensuously immediate art as "kitsch" invited its own obsolescence in a culture increasingly dominated by young people, a culture indifferent to the stuffy categories of "serious" or "frivolous" or "ephemeral" or "commercial."

The affluent society that depended on social repression as its guiding principle spawned a generation that took affluence for granted and Dionysian hedonism as an ideal. The ideologically gridlocked 1950s fairly begged for a thoroughgoing cultural high colonic. The new generation had a long agenda of pleasures and criticalities, a fresh constellation of culture heroes, and, in the universities, its own self-critique as the Society of the Spectacle and commodity-centered capitalism produced a bedazzling richness of contradictions.

The short version of the Abstract Expressionist finale runs that transitional artists like Larry Rivers, Robert Rauschenberg, and Jasper Johns, while sensitive to the atmospheric changes in American society, stressed figurative content at a time when the strategies of AbEx were losing their purchase on public attention. The public for art has always been relatively small, even when the publicity promoting art has been big.

Jasper Johns's 1964 sculpmetal work *The Critic Sees*, in which human mouths appear behind a pair of eyeglass lenses, can be read as a commentary on the dominating role of formalist critics in the artmaking of the previous generation. This jarring piece of bronzed sculpture, showing lips and teeth where one expects to see eyeballs, suggests rather unequivocally that the formalist critics who had supported Abstract Expressionism saw with their mouths and judged works of art on the basis of their own critical pronouncements rather than the intrinsic qualities of the works themselves.

As discussed earlier, the major power brokers Clement Greenberg and Harold Rosenberg, as well as other critics, advocated nonfigurative, "spontaneously" generated painting and highly schematized, geometrically precise-looking abstraction; such art supposedly emanated subjectivity, soulfulness, the heroically turbulent interiority of the artist, and made vivid the implicit mysticism in the painter's relationship to painting that connected with archetypes, mythology, "the eternal." The artists they celebrated were besotted by their own importance and as vigilant as raptors about maintaining their status.

The audacious, contemplative, iconographic, outward-looking, but still very painterly work of Johns and Rauschenberg, which often included—spectacularly, in Rauschenberg's case—elements of sculpture and "found" objects gussied up with smears and splashes of paint (a stuffed goat girdled with a car tire, a mattress and bed used as a canvas, and so on), achieved some respectful acknowledgment from the Abstract Expressionists. In one well-known nod, de Kooning gave his consent to Rauschenberg's erasure of a de Kooning drawing as a conceptual foray. The superannuating Pop Art wave that Johns and Rauschenberg enabled before the end of the '50s served to demoralize the macho mandarins of the Cedar Tavern. They had been confident as they surveyed their swaggering ownership of Art Beach even as the sand was being swept from under their feet. The high tide of artistic anarchy was upon them before they really understood what had occurred. Therefore, to say that Pop Art represented everything they hated would be a gross understatement. And for many years no Pop artist was more despised by the AbEx men's club than Andy Warhol, whose work brazenly excluded the whole idea of artistic subjectivity, "self-expression," and the painting as a sacrosanct, unique object and whose personality similarly refuted the idea of the artist as someone with an urgent personal stake in what he committed to a painting or wrought in other media.

Warhol infuriated de Kooning, among others, by claiming only to paint ordinary things that he happened to like, and by painting them in the starkest, most personally uninflected manner, by making art in the easiest way he possibly could: he wasn't struggling with inner demons, or wresting from paint any sort of transcendental truth, and his work seemed to lampoon the whole idea of artmaking as something intrinsically difficult that carried any risk of failure. For Warhol, the art object didn't even have to be made by the artist—he just had to attach his signature to it after it came off the assembly line. Warhol did, in fact, put immense labor into his own work and, generally speaking, made most of it himself (with physical help from assistants), but he tauntingly denied doing so whenever he was interviewed. That he intensely cared about what he was doing was a fact he would almost never admit, and certainly never in public; such an admission would have betrayed that he had any emotions about anything, which would have compromised the public image he carefully crafted, for self-protection as well as to stoke its immense fascination for the art press, the mass media, and the elite that would buy his work. Other Pop artists were more than happy to explain themselves and what they were trying to do. By withholding such explanations—or, more accurately, emitting clipped, comical, epigrammatic, and contradictory substitutes for more highfalutin pronouncements—Warhol became the most rarefied and famed exemplar of Pop Art and its only real national, finally international, celebrity.

TWO

One artist who brought a jazz-inflected dissonance into the precincts of the New York School and its polemics has been underrated in histories of the era. Viva once dubbed Larry Rivers "the gag man of modern art," and besides being a virtuoso painter, he was: in the Cedar Tavern bust-up-the-bar crowd, Rivers was the least swaggering, least didactic of artists, with broad interests in far-out departures from established artistic practices. If the formerly non-objective painters looked to "neo" figurative painting with the surface tropes of AbEx, Rivers's "history paintings"—among them *Washington Crossing the Delaware*, *Friendship of America and France* (Kennedy and de Gaulle), *The History of the Russian Revolution*, and *Dutch Masters*— were not what they had in mind.

In his broad parodies of the "history paintings" of the academic past, Rivers used the gestural, painterly techniques of the New York School, whose solemnity he treated as an irresistible target for deflating visual jokes, saturated with uninhibited Jewish humor (Lenny Bruce humor), told on canvases more expansive and less portentously ironic than the "serious" productions of Robert Rauschenberg and Jasper Johns.

While Johns and Rauschenberg were prime movers away from AbEx, Rivers was the only talent who comfortably navigated the yawning gap between the New York School and the realm of Pop, socially as well as aesthetically. His antic personality and his finesse at avoiding scraps over other people's hobbyhorses made him welcome everywhere. While de Kooning once screamed into Warhol's face that Andy had "destroyed art," Rivers partied with Warhol and paid appreciative attention to his work.

Rivers was candidly perverse, radically open-minded. His background as a jazz musician, his service in the army, his exposure to the New York social strata alien to the Cedar Tavern crowd, his polymorphic openness to new experiences, gave him something of Duchamp's detachment from what came and went in art fashion; regardless of Rivers's skills as draftsman, painter, and sculptor of objects, he never took himself too seriously. When Pop Art popped onto the scene, Rivers had already "gotten the joke" long before the art establishment.

THREE

The myth of Pop Art runs that isolated, disparately spread-about artists in New York, working in isolation from each other, suddenly began producing recognizably related works, and Pop "just sort of happened." Johns and Rauschenberg had made the world safe for Pop by incorporating mass media images, bits of stray effluvia from the American junk heap. The subversive depictions of targets, maps, flags, sculpted body parts, a goat with an auto tire around its midsection, and other combine paintings, incorporating silkscreened repros from magazines and newspapers, blended with emphatic "evidence of the hand" in the application of paint and encaustic, provided an essential transition between abstraction and Pop.

This is both true and false. Johns and Rauschenberg were forerunners of Pop Art in New York, and some histories refer to them as Pop artists. They made much of the work of the New York School appear stale, self-important, humorless, and boring, but it was anyway.

Johns's work was austerely controlled, and Rauschenberg's baroque in its combinatory audacity. Both were cerebral, aloof, reluctant to prescribe or endorse any particular method of reading their works. But both were forthcoming about their unwillingness to get "lost in the painting," to relinquish control of its elements. The "look" of gestural accident was simply a visual ingredient in a work rather than unplanned discovery. In other words, everything about the work was *calculated*, however spontaneous it might appear at first glance.

While Johns's encaustic brushwork *looked* the way the surfaces of AbEx paintings were supposed to look, its execution was a calculated mimesis, producing the opposite of a projected inner world: Johns inventoried what the eye encountered "out there," including the techniques of non-objective paintings.

For Rauschenberg, Abstract Expressionism's spontaneous slathers and drips could be appropriated as mannerisms, combined with commercial paint color samples, bits of found detritus, and silkscreened details from historical fine art paintings and newspaper photographs; he transformed the overheated rhetorical visuals of AbEx into visual pastiche and assemblage; his work was cool, distanced from the emotional associations of its imagery, droll in an assertively outlandish way. Nevertheless, the couple (they were a couple) paid obeisance to their predecessors and thus were assimilated into the canonical hierarchy—certainly more quickly than Larry Rivers, though some early Rivers works were purchased by museums.

One explanation of Pop's earliest influences can be found in scattered writings of the artist and filmmaker Jack Smith, whose almost secret public performances and pioneering film *Flaming Creatures* had a powerful influence on Robert Wilson, Andy Warhol, the Theater of the Ridiculous, and other theatrical and visual innovators. Noting that Americans expected art to be "heavy," ponderous, and solemn, Smith argued that, on the contrary, the most delightful and profound art was "light," capricious, improvisational, saturated with illogic, chaos, and humor, and that it freely employed the most flamboyant kitsch pop culture had to offer. Smith's theory seems to be supported by the ease with which ponderous art was accepted by critics and audiences and by the automatic dismissal of works containing irony, humor, and a sense of the ephemeral. The art establishment had been locked into Greenburg's opinions regarding high culture and taste. Smith sought to pick the lock.

FOUR

Pop Art didn't spring from the brow of anyone and splash down as ceiling leaks in scattered coldwater studios all over Manhattan. Pop had its own extensive pedigree, dating from the predominantly European phenomena of the early twentieth century, Cubist collages and Dada. Its first cousins were Kurt Schwitters, Marcel Duchamp, Francis Picabia, Man Ray, Morton Livingston Schamberg, John Heartfield, Sophie Taeuber, Emmy Hemmings, Hugo Ball, Marcel Janco, and Viking Eggeling—a lineage into which Johns and Rauschenberg, Pop or not, can be fitted. Like the Dadaists, Pop artists appropriated familiar bits of "found reality," including advertisements, commercial lettering, product logos, newspaper headlines, train tickets, and other flotsam and jetsam of mass culture. It is possible that these references were not as well understood by postwar American art audiences, at least not at first.

It happened that many artists whose works had obvious affinities were discovered by art dealers in search of the new between 1955 and 1965—Jim Dine, James Rosenquist, Claes Oldenburg, Edward Kienholz, Tom Wesselmann, Ray Johnson, Mel Ramos, Ed Ruscha, Marisol, Joe Goode, Robert Indiana, John Chamberlain, George Segal, and Roy Lichtenstein. These artists could be readily linked to new developments in European painting and sculpture, to work by Martial Raysse, Arman, Alain Jacquet, Wolf Vostell, Michaelangelo Pistoletto, Gerhard Richter, Joseph Beuys, and the British Pop artists. This critical mass could be attributed to the artists' responses not only to AbEx but to each other's incorporation of mass media content and materials like neon and billboard advertising into their artwork and to political and cultural shifts in the society at large. A public mystified by abstract painting viscerally responded to imagery and materials familiar from the wider world around them, even when that same public felt unqualified to judge whether this new wave of iconography was truly "art" in an acceptable sense, or merely the activity of a surpassingly large number of eccentric pranksters. When the elite that decided such things began attaching large cultural meaning and, more importantly, cash value to these works, however, the general public—never much concerned about art in the first place—learned to accept the idea that "high art" had shifted into an altogether less intimidating, more instantly understood mode.

It isn't clear who coined the term, but "Pop" as a specific type of new art most likely acquired its name from critic Lawrence Alloway. Its point was first made by a 1956 collage by British artist Richard Hamilton entitled *Just what is it that makes today's homes so different, so appealing?* Hamilton's zany, overstuffed travesty depicts a basement apartment living room, its interior replete with a woman in pearls on a TV screen chatting on the phone, while a "real" woman in nipple pasties and a lampshade on her head strikes a semirecumbent pose on a sofa; another woman, culled from an ad, in a red dress, vacuum-cleans the upper reaches of a gold-carpeted entrance staircase. Another lampshade incorporates the hood emblem of a Ford automobile. A canned ham stands totemlike on a coffee table. A black-and-white, reel-to-reel tape recorder rests on the floor. A Formica sheet that resembles a black-and-white Jackson Pollock leans at a precarious angle against one wall, mysteriously supporting the legs of a second sofa and an end table. The framed cover of a "Young Romance" comic hangs on the wall; through what look like sliding glass windows revealing the street above, a Warners' Theater features Al Jolson's *The Jazz Singer*.

The most instantly attention-grabbing image in Hamilton's collage is that of a Mr. Universe–type bodybuilder in a jock strap, his right hand gripping an enormous, phallic Tootsie Pop stick, the round candy end enclosed in red-and-yellow wrapping. The word pop on the candy wrapper pops out from the center of the picture.

Hamilton's *Just what is it*... has the jumbled horror vacuui effect, stuffed with iconography that Pop artists would adopt as singular, hyperinflated subjects: comics, including dialogue balloons, candies and sweets, parodistic nudes, evocations of early Hollywood, Abstract Expressionist devices detached from their "sincere" contexts, ad design, a clash of sign systems.

Rauschenberg, Rivers, Edward Kienholtz, and Jim Dine mined much of the same territory that Hamilton and other British artists (Eduardo Paolozzi, R. J. Kitaj, David Hockney, Peter Blake) did at roughly the same time. If Hamilton's collage seems originary, it's because of the strategic placement of the Tootsie Pop wrapper, which seems to protrude from the bodybuilder's groin.

This is conscious high camp, recalling the embrace by many art movements of the negatively aimed words and phrases that hostile critics used to dismiss them. It seems natural, if not factual, that Hamilton's outrageous positioning of pop in *Just what is it . . .* decided the new art's lasting appellation.

PART TWO

Figment

chapter four

INSIDE ANARCHY'S RISING TIDE

ONE

SIXTIES YOUTH CULTURE WAS AN AMALGAM OF DESIRES, utopian wishes, and schemes of self-liberation. The tide that washed Pop Art onto America's shore also brought with it anarchy and militant avatars. These avatars advocated for drastic forms of dissent and personal escape from the prescriptive life itinerary of their class—overwhelmingly, the up-to-then-complacent middle class. The comfortable middle was a class that was completely alien to Andy Warhol's experience; for Andy, the extremes of American life, and the extremes of art, were the natural subjects of his work as well as the sources of his sensibility.

Pop Art coincided with the materialization of a New Left that was contemptuous of the Old Left's polemics and its failure to affect the country's domestic and foreign policies. Incinerated draft cards, mass marches and demonstrations, race riots and love-ins youthquaked the mellow acquiescence of the Eisenhower years. Some understood only retrospectively that they had lived as much in fear of nuclear annihilation as of sudden affluence during the Eisenhower years. Yet the high hopes for progressive change that blew in with the Kennedy administration swiftly blew back out. JFK's brief government ratcheted up existing threats of annihilation and an endless Cold War against the Soviet Union, using brinksmanship tactics in response to crises—the airlifts into divided Berlin, the Cuban Missile Crisis, the Bay of Pigs Invasion. JFK was his father's son in many ways besides satyriasis—for example, vis-à-vis the civil rights movement: every concession to it was made grudgingly, for politically expedient reasons.

A White House that invited Robert Lowell and Norman Mailer to dinner was simultaneously prepared to blast humanity into nonexistence to ensure "American supremacy." The physical attractiveness of the First Family transmitted an opposite message of reformist energy and steadfast efforts toward a safer world. John and Jackie Kennedy were, as many knew at the time, "with it" in ways no earlier American ruling couple had ever been.

At this historical juncture, often referred to as the New Frontier, Warhol's *Soup Cans* insinuated themselves into the cultural mix like deftly placed time bombs.

TWO

The emerging Pop artists all arrived at their defining subject matter by considering the American scene and its contents. Claes Oldenberg had devised his "soft" sculptures of objects like typewriters and "hard," jumbo-scaled office erasers; James Rosenquist adapted his experience as a billboard painter to works juxtaposing jet fighters with salon-style hair dryers, atomic blasts with coiled spaghetti and rowing oars; Tom Wesselmann embarked on his Great American Nudes, George Segal on his plaster figures in tableaux, Jim Dine on his "painting objects" of bathrobes, shirts, and neckties embedded in thick skins of uniformly colored paint.

Warhol's "Pop statement" began with a sequence of hard-edged, black-and-white paintings of bakelite telephones, Coke bottles, storm window ads, and similarly "naked" subjects—culminating in the supreme, cryptic obviousness of the *Campbell's Soup Cans*.

The genesis of these works is complicated. Warhol initially worried that the stripped-down look of his first important Pop paintings wouldn't look like art without some slather of assertive brushwork in them. The unexhibited, "arty" early versions of these pictures still exist and are probably worth millions. But the strong suit of the blunt, completely impersonal Coke bottle was, precisely, that it didn't look like art. It presented itself as art, without any apologetics to the New York School. They claimed their own space as art and successfully determined what art would look like now.

These transitional works were themselves a dramatic break with the ornate whimsy of Warhol's commercial and noncommercial drawings; the emergence of Pop Art in the work of post–Abstract Expressionist artists revived Warhol's determination to break through into "fine art." He feared missing his moment. He was virtually the last major Pop artist to be "discovered."

Warhol had never abandoned his ambition: it had waited in abeyance. He'd lacked a way into the established gallery system of the 1950s, although he had been involved with the underground poetry and per-formance scene in downtown Manhattan, an excited witness to the largely unpublicized realm of little art and poetry magazines, beatnik readings, and experimental theater.

The hard-edged paintings were not what Warhol showed Leo Castelli, however, when Ivan Karp, Castelli's assistant at the time, dragged the dealer to Warhol's studio in 1962: what Warhol had on hand were comic strip paintings, with drools and slathery brushwork, and Castelli initially chose not to represent him because they covered essentially the same territory as Roy Lichtenstein, already a client.

The *Soup Cans* are generally credited to the suggestion of Muriel Latow, an art dealer and decorator, who in late 1961 told Warhol he should paint money "or something people see every day, like a Campbell's Soup can." According to Victor Bockris's biography, Andy sent Julia to the supermarket the following day to buy "each of the thirty-two varieties" of the soup and began by making a series of drawings.

The paintings were produced by hand, using stencils and projected slides, and their handmade quality can be seen in the sometimes wobbly lettering and the blank gold medallion in the center of the can's design. Bockris refers to the paintings as "portraits," and this seems exactly right: Warhol's technique invested the cheap manufactured object with the solemn dignity of portraiture.

The appearance of Warhol's *Campbell's Soup Can* paintings at Ivan Karp's Ferus Gallery in Los Angeles on July 9, 1962, ranged evenly along the walls like supermarket merchandise, drew more derision than enthusiasm. A nearby gallery filled its windows with Campbell's soup and offered "the real thing for only 33 cents a can." As biographer Bob Colacello noted, however, "Andy turned ridicule to his advantage. He took a photographer to the supermarket and got his picture taken signing the real thing. The photo was picked up by the Associated Press and wired around the world."[1] (In Colacello's account, the "real" soup cans were displayed in the windows of a supermarket; in several others, they appeared in the windows of the David Stuart Gallery, which was next door to Ferus. Warhol's career is so much a matter of mythology that even simple matters of fact such as this have become muddled from book to book.)

The *Soup Cans* acquired lasting, retroactive notoriety via Warhol's subsequent elephantine output. They were, and still are, confused with the serial silkscreen works Warhol began producing later in industrial quantities. It took many more Warhol products, differently manufactured, for the artist's standout achievement to acquire its symbolic cachet. And Warhol himself crafted an indelible public image that became synonymous with the *Soup Cans.*

The *Soup Can* series condensed, like canned soup, what Pop Art had been seeking. It reflected the unanticipated effects of technological changes on the ways Americans lived after World War II—changes in mores and values created by accelerated consumerism.

THREE

As displayed at the Ferus Gallery, the *Soup Cans*, measuring twenty-by-sixteen inches, executed in synthetic polymer paint on an even white ground, may have resembled a hyper-enlarged supermarket display, but they suggested too a serial montage, like that of the film strip. If you think of the *Soup Cans* as a succession of flavors, they naturally evoke the passage of time best captured on film—the time of consumption, the filmic element of time embedded in everyday life. It is a monotonous element marked by small differences, suggestive of mass production, mass consumption, and waste. The ensemble is, or was, an inventory: Warhol fastidiously obtained a complete list of Campbell's existing varieties from the manufacturer, checking each one off as a painting of it was completed.

The painstaking production of the *Soup Cans* and their release into the world as works of art represented a watershed experience for Warhol and, in time, for American culture. Warhol created a pertly designed window into the abyss, in a sense, erasing the sense of spirituality that earlier generations had associated with art. The viewer was obliged to confront glut: a ceaseless proliferation of objects for sale, objects that defined modern lives as quanta.

In a 1962 statement about an earlier, black-and-white painting, *Storm Door* (1960), Warhol explicitly commented on the imagery best epitomized by the *Soup Cans*: "My image is a statement of the symbols of the harsh, impersonal products on which America is built today. It is a projection of everything that can be bought and sold, the practical but impermanent symbols that sustain us."[2]

Warhol found in the soup can a particularly useful symbology, drawing and painting it in a multiplicity of sizes and conditions: in other serial paintings, such as *100 Cans*, in which all the cans are labeled Beef Noodle; in the painting *200 Cans*, depicting mixed flavors; singly and in groups, with open lids attached like hinges; as crushed cans, dented cans, and cans in small groups arranged in clumplike formations; as cans with the labels sliding off, revealing the mottled tin cylinder beneath; as flattened cans; and as an open can of chicken noodle soup, with the red parts of the label colored in and partly obscured by the can opener, the manual kind that includes a corkscrew. Working from projected photographs, Warhol considered the can as thoroughly as he would the human face.

By portraying this iconic item in both its intact, market-going state and its varying stages of distress from being used and discarded, Warhol in effect charted the life span of a commodity, showing both its utilitarian ubiquity and its "death." Warhol used a broad range of materials—oil paint, watercolor, pencil, press-type, acrylic, silkscreen ink—in his exploration of all the artisanal possibilities at hand to depict essentially the same thing. When Warhol found a subject, he worked it to exhaustion—at times revisiting it when he hit upon a new technique, such as the "Negative" versions of his early work in which the photographic reverse of the image appears—and saved any auxiliary materials used in the process, creating an almost infinite archive of his own activity. In his depiction of the disposable, he accrued an archaeological residue of the objects of his gaze.

Warhol presents us with the container, never the contents: the *Campbell's Soup Cans* "refer" to nourishment, food, the elemental necessity of the life process, but invariably they show the form in which this manna is packaged for consumption, contained within a system of mass production, "drained," in effect, of gratification, presented in a masked and dissembled state that has no emotional affect but rather an optical histrionics.

Warhol's cans demonstrate that modern reality is mediated through the symbolic. They indicate desire (hunger) and the absence of substance (eating), and the mechanized stimulation of desire is arguably their "theme." The inconsequential variations on the container and unrelenting emphasis on monotony and repetition do indeed stress "the practical and impermanent" as the mode of life in a mass society—an idea that can be extended to Warhol's depictions of human faces and bodies, plants and animals, materiality and emotion.

FOUR

There is nothing ambiguous about a soup can. But a painting of a soup can, in 1962, bristled with suggestiveness. It represented, some thought, an indictment of quantity over quality. It could be related to widespread uneasiness with American materialism, its sexual repressiveness, its racism, the ugliness of its cities and towns. It could say: "This is what we eat, and this is what we are."

From a different perspective, the unembellished, flat commercial image, inserted into the "sacred space" of art, was as fresh as a brisk wind, blowing away old ideas about how images affect people and what images compel their attention.

Pop could mean "populist" or "popular," as you preferred.

The equalizing effect of Warhol's technique on the imagery of American popular culture emphasized the omnipresence of media images. The naked, isolated soup cans repudiated the idea of "subjectivity." Everything "outside" became the same thing, in a sense, as a soup can.

Warhol found the perfect metaphor for what was happening in the middle-class world of the affluent society. The *Soup Cans* were insouciant, defiant, impeccably unembellished examples of what novelist William Burroughs had termed "the naked lunch at the end of the newspaper fork," acerbic "no comment" comments on the previous decade's unbearable conformism, emblems of the social and political heterodoxy spreading through American society. They were banal. They were visionary. They were works of obdurate stupidity radiating the aptness of genius. They have never lost their iconic punch, perhaps because they transmuted the banality of a specific, familiar object into a wink of nonconformity—the kind of dissonance and contradiction in which ever-growing masses of people, immersed in an environment indistinguishable from advertising, now live.

Warhol was a protean maker of meaningful images remarkable for their apparent meaninglessness. Their neutrality made the viewer's reaction the true subject of the work. When you looked at a Warhol painting, the painting blankly stared back. Warhol rewired your perception of what you already knew. He forced your attention on the elaborately constructed nature of society, its labor-intensive artifice, the complex design of images and objects that were taken for granted as "natural." Other Warhol works may have had a greater effect on aesthetic perception than the *Soup Cans*. But no Warhol pictures are "perfect" in the same sense that the *Campbell's Soup Cans* are perfect. Everything else Warhol painted, filmed, tape-recorded, videotaped, photographed, or simply attached his name to carries a vestige of personal idiosyncrasy and "differentness."

The *Soup Can* paintings mocked the importance placed on art by timeless criteria of aesthetics. They scrambled the categories of "major" and "minor," "commercial art" and "fine art." They moved the work of art into the realm of objects previously unperceived as "commodities." The art gallery and the supermarket drew closer together.

The *Soup Can* effect was not to rescue American banalities from banality, but to give banality itself value. After some initial hesitance about what he was doing, Warhol never wavered.

The *Soup Cans* were of their time, and about their time. Perhaps their most salient quality is that, unlike other Pop Art paintings, they are "mute," stark, and factual, deriving whatever irony they possess from a receptive viewer, expressive of nothing and nobody in a way that no previous paintings ever were.

F I V E

Early resistance to Warhol's brand of Pop Art undoubtedly owed much to the air of effeminate blankness he presented to the art press and the public. Even before launching himself into filmmaking of a provocatively static, then blatantly joke-pornographic type, he had become synonymous with an "underground" of rampant drug use and sexual polymorphism; his flair for self-promotion guaranteed that this spilled beyond the pages of art magazines into those of tabloid newspapers.

All the same, Warhol could not be avoided as a key practitioner of Pop Art and, as such, the subject of a great deal of formalist art criticism that avoided any mention of the louche, faggoty associations that were rife in his production. The saturnalian aspects of his films, once they became "talkies," were said to be exemplary of a kind of voyeurism assimilable to art history, a mirror of society's underbelly that implicitly distanced the already calculatedly distanced Warhol from what he was recording.

In recent years a lot of polemical energy has gone into "reclaiming" Warhol as a homosexual artist, as if he had ever pretended to be anything else. This kind of polemic is unobjectionable—indeed, it is valuable in an era when gay issues might be considered the last frontier in the struggle for civil rights. At times this kind of critical writing can itself become reductive—for example, in the case of Warhol's installation, on the facade of the New York State Pavilion at the 1964 World's Fair, of *Thirteen Most Wanted Men*, twenty-five uniformly sized, silkscreen-on-masonite panels bearing mug shots of criminals.

Warhol probably intended the title of this work as a double entendre—the men depicted may have been "wanted" by the law, but were also wanted, at least in some cases, as objects of sexual interest. But it seems to me that the work was primarily intended as a subversion of everything a World's Fair is designed to showcase: the most positive and "advanced" features of participating nations.

The mural was banned, either by commissioning architect Philip Johnson or on orders from Governor Nelson Rockefeller. Warhol offered to replace the panels with an equal number of identical portraits of planning commissioner Robert Moses, whom Warhol drolly affected to admire; the idea was promptly rejected. Warhol then had the mural painted over with aluminum house paint. An interesting statement in itself: a shiny nothing.

Perhaps the political subversiveness of *Thirteen Most Wanted Men* is inextricably tied to its sexual subtext; in the early 1960s, Warhol was flaunting his interest in gay subject matter without inhibition. In his later career, the confrontative expression of alternative sexuality outlived its usefulness. It no longer carried any shock value and reaped no particular rewards in terms of publicity—in other words, it had performed its function for Warhol's idiosyncratic advancement as a media star and lucrative artist. In the '70s, when transvestites and underground sex clubs were objects of interest for the monied elite, Warhol produced plenty of works depicting drag queens, male genitalia, and sex; by then, however, his bread and butter consisted of portrait commissions from the ultrawealthy, specialized print editions of endangered animal species or "Ten Portraits of Jews of the Twentieth Century," and the kind of subject matter he'd broken into Pop Art with: consumer products. In the 1980s, when the Campbell Soup Company introduced a line of its product in boxes, Warhol created a whole new series of silkscreen paintings immortalizing *them*.

SIX

Irving Blum's offer to show the seminal thirty-two *Campbell's Soup Can* paintings at the Ferus Gallery in Los Angeles and his later determination to keep them together as a set—one of the most lucrative decisions in the history of contemporary art—obliged Blum to buy several canvases back from collectors who'd paid $100 for each; Blum, whom Warhol charged $1,000 in monthly installments, for the entire series, eventually sold the original set to MoMA for $15 million, while a single *Soup Can*, not part of the series, went at auction not long ago for $11 million.

The vertiginous outpouring of serial works commencing with Warhol's *Soup Cans* made "Pop" a blanket term for all kinds of art practices. The Pop artists were looking for a new approach to things, and for the things themselves—in making a stylistic break from the painterly strictures of the New York School, they were searching for subject matter that reflected the outer world rather than the artist's interiority. The growing perception that there was no real difference between the artist's interiority and the outer world was something Warhol had no trouble articulating:

> It doesn't matter what you do. Everybody just goes on thinking the same thing, and every year it gets more and more alike. Those who talk about individuality the most are the ones who most object to deviation, and in a few years it may be the other way around. Some day everybody will think just what they want to think, and then everybody will probably be thinking alike; that seems to be what is happening.[3]

To say that the Ferus Gallery show was derisively greeted by the critical establishment would be misleading. It was scarcely noticed by the critical establishment; only later, after Warhol had shown the *Soup Can* pictures and other Pop paintings elsewhere in group shows of Pop Art and had done other one-artist shows of other works, did the *Soup Cans* become objects of critical scrutiny.

Reviewing a show at the Pasadena Art Museum called "New Paintings of Common Objects" later in 1962, Jules Langsner wrote, in the September 1962 issue of *Art International*: "A can of *Campbell Soup* by Andy Warhol . . . initially rivets the viewer's attention . . . by removing the mundane object from its ordinary surroundings and enormously increasing its scale. The initial shock, however, wears off in a matter of seconds, leaving one as bored with the painting as with the object it presents."[4]

Michael Fried, writing in the December 1962 issue of *Art International*, was similarly dismissive: "I am not at all sure that even the best of Warhol's work can much outlast the journalism on which it is forced to depend."[5]

Artists had mixed reactions. Donald Judd, writing in *Arts* in January 1963, observed that "Warhol's work is able but general. It certainly has possibilities, but it is so far not exceptional."[6] Los Angeles–based artist John Baldessari, who saw the original Ferus Gallery show, recently told Philip Larratt-Smith in an interview: "I remember they were all in a row and as I recall they were sitting on a very narrow shelf. I liked the matter-of-factness of it, that they were just like products in a supermarket, with all the cans lined up. . . . It did sort of resonate; what I liked about it was, Wow, I guess he thinks he can get away with this."[7]

As Pop Art and Warhol burgeoned as phenomena, criticism likewise proliferated, as did misunderstandings about what had been shown at the Ferus Gallery in the first place. In light of Warhol's subsequent works, many assumed that the *Soup Cans* had been produced with photographic silkscreens; other opinionators who knew the *Soup Cans* had been hand-painted regarded them as a flagrant waste of craftsmanship, a flouting not only of "taste" but of art itself—while still others found in them an implacable mystery, an almost hallucinatory heightening of everyday reality.

The *Soup Cans*, to many eyes, embodied the ultimate in "camp sensibility": while the paintings emitted nothing sexually suggestive or homosexually ironic per se, those in the know about Warhol's sexuality (just about everybody as Warhol's public image became ubiquitous) interpreted the glorification of such aesthetically questionable objects, presented in utterly deadpan fashion, as a variant of the same "insider" hilarity as such camp objects as Tiffany lamps and cha-cha heels—their presentation as "art" was thought to constitute a kind of absurdist excess different from other Pop Art, something that could be construed as a form of sly, gestural homosexual signaling.

Again, it seems necessary to stress that Warhol's *Campbell's Soup Can* series, however crucially it represents a turning point in American culture, cannot be considered in isolation from the rapid and vast proliferation of other Warhol works that seemed to flood the American art scene in the 1960s: the silkscreen paintings of celebrities, the sculptures, the films, the phenomenon of the Factory—all embellished the *Soup Cans* with a retroactive mythic quality, heavily tinted by the brazen sexual "degeneracy" that the Warhol scene (no other Pop artist had "a scene") came to exemplify.

chapter five

MASS PRODUCTION

ONE

FROM 1963 ONWARD, ANDY WARHOL BEGAN MORPHING from a professional artist whose background was based in advertising into a professional creative celebrity, one whose destiny was determined by a series of calculated risks. Like the Industrial Revolution titans who realized that mass production was the key to personal wealth, Warhol relied on mass production not only to make a name for himself as an artist, but as a means of making money and lots of it.

TWO

Immediately after the *Soup Cans*, Warhol began using photographic silkscreens to make his paintings, a rapid means of multiplying his output. No two silkscreen works are exactly the same. The reusable screens, ostensibly intended to generate many identical images, introduced arbitrary, painterly variations and intriguing singularities that the *Soup Can* period had seemingly repudiated. Such was the paradox of mechanization: individuated differences "slipped in," revealing themselves only through almost microscopic scrutiny. Clogs, uneven pressure on the screen press, and irregularities in the canvas or the primer coat created gaps between serially contiguous images, areas of lighter and darker color, shifting degrees of legibility, and other inconsistencies. These inconsistencies were deliberate (deliberately allowed to stay in the pictures, that is), calculated, in the sense that they could be counted on to appear, and sloppy, like the slosh of one mechanical process over another, a liquid mopped over a photographic image, introduced into Warhol's simulations for the evocation of motion picture film passing through a projector, the image flickering from near-blackness to an oversaturation that makes the image a ghostly nimbus.

He may have said that he wanted to be a machine, but with regard to his work he only acted like one in the sense that he never stopped working. He only partially ascribed to composer John Cage's dictum to welcome the operations of chance: Warhol knew which accidents were "right" for his work and which ones wouldn't do. He brought the idea of aesthetic choice to bear on procedures that seemed a refutation of aesthetics, and on paintings that mocked the art of painting. Mockery and mimicry were fused, and most significantly, the reproduction and the original were inextricably mixed together.

THREE

After JFK's assassination in November 1963, the *Soup Can* paintings acquired a punchy and even edgier association with a full-blown social upheaval; Warhol personally, in a vertiginously short time, became associated with dark, unsavory things on the nether edge of "the counterculture." America had always selectively repressed its own history and asserted its self-evident virtue after every self-inflicted disaster, but the JFK killing was touted as "the day America lost its innocence." At that frozen moment, the *Soup Can* paintings were among the most conspicuous visible manifestations of "American culture," evidence of a society in upheaval, and they attached themselves to an extreme turning point in American self-awareness.

In response to the assassination, Warhol immediately embalmed the iconography of collective grief and mourning in a series of silkscreens of Jackie Kennedy before and after the assassination, producing a kind of frieze of shock—the shock of the irremediable, an event recognizable by everyone as "a turning point" in our collective history.

What Warhol pictured didn't necessarily evoke the emotional turmoil of the Kennedy assassination. His silkscreens of the First Lady in mourning, instead, recorded "the iconic moments" that had already registered powerfully with the mass public and functioned as afterimages, residue, instantly historicized phosphenes. They were directly transported from mass media into fine art, translated into art from powerful news photographs, like the suicides, car accidents, race riots, and other images of "death and disaster" that Warhol turned to after picturing consumer products, labels, and money. None of these images "spoke" about the things they pictured; they processed the way reality had been made to look already by the camera—and someone else's camera at that.

The dissociation of image from reality, the privileging of images over reality, symptomatic of an affectlessness invariably found in sociopaths, is a major theme in Andy Warhol's work. (It's also the prevailing character of American life today.) Warhol's pictures are often conflated with an endorsement of affectlessness, partly because the self-protective public image Warhol constructed, like that of a movie star, was laconic-bordering-on-mute, recessive, not so much aloof as dazed, as if blinded by flashbulbs (which he often was). And partly because Warhol, growing up homosexual in the '30s and '40s, had shame and desire dueling in his psyche and had finally forced a truce between them with a Zen-like indifference clause written into it: too many emotions, too much emotion, would have been risky to his life, his art, his career.

The paintings and silkscreens of Marilyn Monroe and Liz Taylor (when she was thought to be at the brink of death from pneumonia in London) and the images of the Kennedy assassination existed to serve Andy's absorption with celebrity, yet he sometimes wanted to memorialize the anonymous and forgotten. In a 1966 interview with Gretchen Berg in the *East Village Other*, commenting on the "Death and Disaster" series, Warhol said:

> The death series I did was divided into two parts: the first on famous deaths and the second on people

nobody ever heard of and I thought people should think about them sometimes: the girl who jumped off the Empire State Building or the ladies who ate the poisoned tuna fish and people getting killed in car crashes. It's not that I feel sorry for them, it's just that people go by and it doesn't really matter to them that someone unknown was killed so I thought it would be nice for these unknown people to be remembered by those who, ordinarily, wouldn't think of them.[1]

However blandly and coldly stated, for Warhol to embark on the "Death and Disaster" paintings at all reflects a scared awareness of other people's unhappiness or bad luck and his own terror of death. The latter he dissembled with his lobster shell of emotional vacancy when other people died and with his refusal to exhibit any aggrieved or strongly negative feelings at all.

FOUR

With ascendancy came the need for continual change. Warhol realized that the best way to keep an audience interested was to keep them guessing about what would come next. The techniques might be the same, or similar, but the subject matter, invariably drawn from the iconography of commerce and mass media, changed, often capitalizing on whatever celebrity figures or sensational events the culture had fixated on. Warhol, increasingly a focus of mass media attention himself, whimsically adapted his self-presentation and responses to interviewers to "explain" his work using the fewest number of words possible. He was a master of the evasive reply, the oracular-sounding yet empty one-sentence response, and the fact that he never said anything negative about anything led people to believe he was putting them on—which, in all likelihood, he was.

Within his immense oeuvre, all sorts of internal contradictions render sweeping generalizations on such matters moot. In the books he wrote in collaboration with Pat Hackett and others, one finds strikingly altered accounts of the same events, clashing characterizations of the same people, and a multiplicity of Andy Warhols—not in the ordinary sense that everyone has different moods, changes of opinion, and more than one way of regarding the world, but rather in the sense of expressing different parts of himself at different periods, presenting the image of himself best suited to a particular moment in the culture's rapidly shifting zeitgeist.

One can't question Warhol's "sincerity" in any of these incarnations, since each is a highly speculative construct carrying that ring of falsity with which Warhol imbued the truth. Often it works brilliantly. The shelf of books Warhol produced is considerable, and their oscillating quantities of revelation and with-holding suggest that Warhol himself was a series of Warhols, superficially identical with himself, but on closer inspection less and less the same person from one book to the next (or one interview to the next, or one art practice to the next). He imported himself into the image world as much as he could, and his public passivity mimicked the malleability of images—again, as a sort of insulation against death and emotional suffering.

He was too intelligent to really believe in this strat-agem; still, his image(s) did protect him from much of what he didn't want in his life. The pictures he made stared down his desires, but likewise acted as purga-tives. One thing he didn't want in his life was to actu-ally eat Campbell's soup, since he'd had it for lunch every day throughout twenty years of grinding poverty. One of Warhol's Factory familiars recalls that Andy hated Campbell's soup. Making an artistic reputation and a fortune on it was both Warhol's homage to, and revenge on, Campbell's soup.

FIVE

Warhol's self-control was preternatural. Eventually, people with precious little control of themselves gravitated to him as to a sort of high priest or magically endowed parent who could impart importance and a sense of direction to their inner chaos. Most were Catholics, afflicted with free-range guilt and a need to confess and receive absolution. Warhol's films, as well as the social scene that evolved at the Factory, made instant celebrities of the people who ganged around him. His milieu became indissociable from himself, a kind of collective mask or screen projected through his films and the voyeurism of the mass media.

Warhol had the ability to bestow a public image on people the public might never otherwise have heard of. In American society, having an image was steadily becoming more rewarding than being a person; people have problems, but images just have spectators. The most adroit and clever of Warhol's cohorts and groupies managed to make their problems into their images in a compelling way. Neuroticism became a lively asset rather than a liability.

When people think of Andy Warhol, they see a plurality, an assortment of muzzy pictures of personalities swirling around him, pictures in which Warhol himself is practically invisible—though never quite. His studio, christened "the Factory" by Billy Name (who covered the entire place in silver at Warhol's request), became an almost public space where high and low, rich and poor, powerful and powerless, mainstream famous and underground famous, the beautiful and the bizarrely beautiful, mingled in a continuous saturnalia where all social categories became leveled, interchangeable, and irrelevant, much as class and race differences evaporated in gay bars. The Factory embodied Andy's fascination with glamour, high style, and celebrity, especially in close proximity to the trashy, the outlandish, the faintly criminal, and the borderline psychotic. His work mirrors this fascination, but simultaneously evokes the only inescapable link between everyone who came and went and everyone he painted and filmed: the inevitable end of all tomorrow's parties.

SIX

Remembering my own first glimpse of Andy Warhol's image in 1964, in an art magazine photograph of Andy and Edie Sedgwick in a Philadelphia museum, mobbed on a spiral staircase by chanting fans, it's almost impossible to believe that since that frozen moment the figure in the photograph has become, in many discourses, "the most important artist of the second half of the twentieth century," perhaps even "the most important artist of the twentieth century," and, quite bluntly, "the artist who changed everything."

These phrases come tripping to the tongue, and one could trip over one's tongue repeating them. We've heard them so often that we no longer question what they mean. Warhol "changed the way we perceive the world around us." He "made us see reality in a different way." He "completely changed American culture." He may, for that matter, have changed all culture, for all time, through an epidemic form of alchemy.

There could hardly be a more comprehensive book on the Edie Sedgwick legend than Jean Stein's *Edie*, but the image of Andy-and-Edie continues, like the *Campbell's Soup Can* paintings, to operate as visual shorthand for an unrepeatable watershed moment in American cultural history. In 1964 Warhol's life was becoming a narrative. Edie Sedgwick, the following year's "It Girl," became an important episode of the narrative in which the artist appeared in public with his double. She was, in terms of social background and upbringing, his opposite, born to riches in a dysfunctional but New England aristocratic family, and indelibly beautiful, the original waif. She offered refinement, fragility, delicacy with a pedigree, which validated Warhol's own delicacy (and reflected a type of pedigree, like moonlight, on him). They didn't look alike, but dressed alike, wore the same hair color, and shared the quality of ambiguity, unreadableness. Edie completed Andy Warhol in a new way, which made them a new type of power couple: together, they spelled a runic inscription that was all presence, all absence. Edie's death in 1971 (the ultimate absence) elevated the mythology that surrounded them. No other could replace Edie.

Perhaps the strain of being a perpetual implacable presence wore him down over time: Warhol once replaced himself by sending actor Allen Midgette to impersonate him at college lectures; at some juncture, he let it be known that he was having a robot of himself constructed. The idea of replacing himself with a double, or cloning himself, was utterly consistent with Warhol's frequent assertion that anyone could do his paintings, that one could know everything about him by looking at the surfaces of his work, that there was nobody behind any of it; his famous statement that he wanted to be a machine underscored the techniques of mechanical reproduction with which he generated his art.

SEVEN

The sheer volume of work that Warhol intended to produce created the need to build a framework of pseudo-industrial processes.

Warhol often asked people what he should paint; he wrote that he saw no difference between asking friends for ideas and finding them by looking at magazines. But which people he asked, why he asked which specific person, and who actually suggested a particular idea are reported differently throughout the Warhol literature. The attribution of Warhol's ideas to other people seems, in many cases, inconsistent with Warhol's personality. Whether he asked one person or ten people what he should do, Warhol probably listened to everybody and then did what he'd wanted to in the first place.

The studio assistant system flourished at the Factory as Warhol relegitimized and expanded the Renaissance practice of leaving parts of a work, or the whole thing, in the hands of others; to "make" a work could mean simply to conceive it and approve its execution by assistants. In reality, the atelier system of painting continued after the Renaissance right up into the present day. Warhol merely made it familiar to the general public, which had never had any close knowledge of how it worked. (Given the traffic in and out of the Factory, Warhol never signed anything until it was sold; unless it was signed, he hadn't officially made it.)

Warhol didn't really take his cue from the Renaissance, however, but from Hollywood. He was the Irving Thalberg of art, involved in decisive ways in the products issued with his name attached (though Thalberg often left his producer's credit off the films he supervised), leaving the fabrication, the filming, the magazine editing, or whatever the physical job was in other people's hands, to a varying extent.

Warhol's meshing of mechanical reproduction with "the original" generated vast quantities of artwork of varying quality. This became a nightmare for his dealers. His repudiation of the "handmade" also made for a commercially detrimental surplus of saleable works.

His fusion of painting with printmaking and photography, the droll indifference to emerging conventions within Pop Art and other practices, in effect, his unencumbered approach to subject matter and materials, guaranteed ubiquity and cast a shadow on his reputation.

One of the daunting tasks facing the curators and custodians of Warhol's artistic legacy is sorting out who did what in the production of Warhol's work, especially as it spreads out across numerous collaborative media, including the magazine Warhol founded, *Interview*, still in operation today. Warhol had a strong proprietary interest in what he attached his name to, and the endless-seeming abundance of what he produced will take at least a generation or two to catalog.

As the Warhol apparatus expanded, Warhol himself was, publicly, increasingly spectral and indefinable, and the desperate-sounding torrent of adjectives journalists used to describe him was matched by the desperation of others to get his attention. With the Factory, Warhol animated a situation that took on its own aleatory life, a shifting aggregate of volatile and garrulous personalities that attracted celebrities of all stripes and classes, curators, art dealers, artists—a "democratically" elite crowd, some merely browsing, others performing, all of it swirling around Andy (even if he happened not to be there), but not something he could plausibly control. Billy Name and others, at various times, "directed traffic," kept some people out, let others in, but the general impression of the Factory is one of the best party and the biggest bummer anyone can remember.

Every long-running party has its attrition level, and some eyewitnesses to this one offer a less than enthralled recollection of the Factory, as Mary Woronov recounts:

Aware that the rap of a speed freak had been known to completely dissolve even the polish off silver-ware, we confined these raps to our books. Some people thought of their trip books as art—they weren't. They were reams of useless energy, complete with dizzying diagrams of intricate nothing—except when Andy Warhol happened to be doing the drawing.

That night Andy was drawing noses, before and after nose jobs. When he asked me if I liked it, I didn't answer. Why bother? I knew that the stupid drawing would appear in its silkscreen mode later, worth a fortune.[2]

The souped-up Factory as an ever-reconfigured site of outrageous happenings and obligatory drop-in center where authentic celebrities mixed with an array of human wreckage bore little resemblance to Warhol's earlier studios, which were often located in his own cramped residences—the *Soup Can* paintings, for instance, were painted in Andy's townhouse at 1342 Lexington Avenue. In the early days Warhol had worked with one or more assistants, undistracted by the radios, TVs, and record players he kept running while he worked. The Factory, as the separate studio he rented in 1963 at 231 East Forty-seventh Street quickly became dubbed, was a vaudeville hall or circus, crammed with ever-changing acts, from whose "performers" Warhol frequently extracted material for his work, though much of his time was spent "behind the curtain," backstage, workaholically churning out silkscreens, emerging at times to greet celebrities dropping in or to arrange performers in front of his movie camera, switch it on, and disappear again.

E I G H T

Warhol's initial breakthrough as a painter and sculptor, marked by the rapid assimilation and exhaustion of a broad inventory of images, was followed by the announcement that he was abandoning painting. By the time he launched his 1966 *Silver Clouds*, helium pillows (designed in tandem with Billy Kluver's technological expertise) floating at shifting altitudes in the Castelli Gallery, and the flowers-on-cow wallpaper at Sonnabend Gallery, as farewell gestures, Warhol was famous enough to announce his retirement in the time-honored fashion of his idols when they rested up for a comeback.

By 1965, Warhol had become intensely involved— or uninvolved—in filmmaking. Warhol wanted "to throw lightning," as Billy Name put it—to be someone who was not simply a celebrity, but someone who could confer celebrity on other people by paying attention to them. As Irving Thalberg conferred "quality" on M-G-M product by green-lighting prestigious literary properties, Andy began to make media stars of selected protégés, beginning with beauties like Ivy Nicholson and Baby Jane Holzer, the latter proclaimed "Girl of the Year" in 1964, followed by Edie Sedgwick, the star of his early, Ron Tavel–scripted "talkies."

Warhol's movies had an event quality as they appeared, in rapid succession. The early silents bear close relation to Warhol's paintings: static images, they prescribe their own viewing time and, if watched at their intended length and speed of projection, reveal themselves as nonstatic. An analogy can be made to the flaws, strike-overs, and variegated surfaces of Warhol paintings of identical multiple objects, which only look uniformly fabricated at a superficial glance.

The crypto-narrative talkies, including 1965's *My Hustler*, the following year's *The Chelsea Girls*, 1967's *Imitation of Christ, I, a Man, The Loves of Ondine, Bike Boy*, and *Nude Restaurant*, and 1968's *Lonesome Cowboys, San Diego Surf, Flesh*, and *Blue Movie*, whatever else might be said about them, are among the most audaciously, emphatically spellbinding displays of polymorphic sexuality and verbal frankness in film history, in part because of the camera's, or the director's, disregard for continuity or narrative construction, the inclusion of unintelligible stretches of sound track, the pockets of total silence, the use of stuttering zooms, and, confuting their deliberately amateur qualities, a mixture of innovative and classical framing, the inclusion of synechdotal figures and evocative objects at frame edges, and the improvisatory brilliance of actors provided with the sketchiest story premises to work within (when they remember to).

These films follow the same paradigm as Warhol's "no comment" Pop paintings, with many technical decisions left open to chance, and in them Warhol's invisible presence is weirdly palpable. As one anonymous Superstar told me, "It didn't matter who shot it or who 'directed' it, if Andy was in the room, it was Andy's film." The same actor told me that Andy's only direction to him, ever, was to whisper in his ear: "Too much plot."

NINE

The cult of the proper name has a strong, transformative effect on human psychology. It can, in fact, drastically alter reception of a thing and therefore the meaning of that thing. A Raphael painting accepted as authentic for centuries, if suddenly discovered to be the work of a "minor" artist mistakenly attributed to Raphael, becomes something else once stripped of the aura of Raphael.

Andy Warhol is one of the few artists of the past hundred years who was able to create a franchise, recognizable by his signature—Walt Disney was another—sufficiently authoritative that regardless of the artist's degree of direct involvement in a work, its appearance under his name turned it into a work by Andy Warhol, infused it with the artist's sensibility, and subtly influenced its manner of creation and presentation.

With Warhol, we confront a mystery of a different order than that of the Raphael painting before and after its attribution changes. For it is possible to identify the extent of other people's contributions to Warhol's art, even to assign complete "authorship" of some works to other people, yet Warhol's name attached, for example, as "producer" of a piece he had little or nothing definite to do with makes that piece feel like a work by Andy Warhol. One could, perhaps, say the same about the Raphael, but what if we knew Raphael didn't paint the picture in the first place?

The heavy element of creative vampirism that Warhol's practice involved is not unique. There have long been artists, writers, musicians, filmmakers, and other wildly talented people with no aptitude or desire to commodify what they make, romantics who repine for the vie bohème and a select community in which they participate as both artists and audiences; likewise, there have always been those, often of lesser talent and greater willfulness, with an eye for the main chance, who cull from the works of others the method, the material, the quiddity of what is "squandered" by a lack of savvy packaging and make it theirs.

The distinction isn't necessarily a simple divide between haplessly self-sabotaging "creators" and opportunistic larcenists. It reflects two opposing philosophical and, if you like, moral viewpoints. The bohemian may crave recognition, and his or her supporters may routinely deplore the exploitation of the bohemian's ideas by commercially successful talents. Behind this lies a utopian wish that artistic endeavors were exempted from the brutal reality of capitalism. In the bohemian artist, both desire and contempt for popularity and material reward produce an ambivalence seldom resolved and usually self-defeating.

Capitalism in its current, all-pervasive form exacerbates the preextant desire for fame and money and ratifies egregious opportunism. Becoming an artist remains a gut imperative for many, but being an artist is as firmly fixed today as "a profession" as any other and, given the potential rewards, often becomes a career choice for people whose real talents may lie entirely elsewhere. Which is not to imply that highly gifted artists can't also be liars and thieves, to put it crudely; an argument can be made that no work of art is made without some model in mind, however sketchy, and the aporias of bohemia, practically speaking, may have purist beauty, but the modicum of survival mechanisms once available to artists on the permanent fringe have evaporated from the very cities to which bohemian artists once gravitated.

Warhol functioned as one of the progenitors of a corporate monoculture and greatly assisted the liquidation of the double culture of below versus above, bohemian obscurity versus celebrity, the dignity of "failure" versus the importance of "success." Even the young artists Warhol cultivated near the end of his life served less as generative collaborators than as people whose celebrity was magnified by their association with Warhol, and from whose association he extracted a "youthful" cachet he had long ceased to radiate himself.

chapter six

THAT ONE PAINTING

ONE

"I SHOULD HAVE JUST KEPT PAINTING THE SOUP CANS," Warhol asseverated many times, knowing he would be remembered for those pictures—and, moreover, remembered for the gesture rather than the object.

Not by art historians and archivists, who would pore over everything Warholian with a microscope, but by the media-dazzled public that consumed soup cans, Coca-Cola, Elizabeth Taylor, and Warhol's mere signature. In that, Warhol could exercise no control at all.

If there is one artist who bears comparison, who made it possible for Warhol to become Warhol, it is

Dada's art star, Marcel Duchamp. Duchamp not only paved the way but drew a concise road map.

Duchamp dispensed with painting and invented the "readymade," the object plucked from the realm of mass-produced objects, presenting it as art by adding his signature to it. A snow shovel, a urinal, a bicycle wheel mounted on a four-legged stool—these objects became "art" because Duchamp selected them, sometimes provided them with a witty title, and presented them as his work.

He met Warhol many times, and Duchamp's conceptual gestures undoubtedly influenced Warhol's practice of presenting reproductions of the manufactured, preexisting image or object as his "work," though there's nothing to suggest that Warhol influenced Duchamp in any way: Duchamp's stock-in-trade was to produce less and less as an artist, and he placidly and no doubt amusedly watched as the objects he'd exhibited many decades earlier, and the thinking behind them, acquired a prophetic cachet for the artists who became important in the 1960s. Warhol simply adapted the idea of the readymade to the hyperproduction of paintings, prints, sculptures, and films that required no editing and no direction.

Marcel Duchamp is said to have "revolutionized art," for those concerned with art. Yet he didn't even call his own activity art, except when applying its Sanskrit meaning "to make." Duchamp made eminent sense: no false modesty, no hubris, only a dry irony applied to an exquisitely limited output.

He neither embraced nor rejected the world as he found it. Like the writer Georges Perec, he played certain games, indulged a kind of artmaking at once transparent and opaque, imposing gamelike limitations on his production. He transformed the accidental and the readymade into concepts that acquired the qualities of repudiation of and finality to art, or to art as it had always been practiced before him.

The only artist Duchamp competed with was Duchamp. His world had room for other artists, with whom he could maintain a generative dialogue. If he struck a pose, it was not that of a celebrity. He simply altered the conceptual terms in which art might be understood—and the word "might" itself places this notion in a provisional realm.

Warhol shares Duchamp's indifference to aesthetic strictures. Warhol's need to control, his cultivation of personal publicity, on the other hand, runs counter to Duchamp's reclusiveness and willingness to relinquish control to accidents of matter and to welcome chance.

Claims for Warhol may be more sweeping, more widely embraced, because, unlike Duchamp, Warhol was infatuated with celebrity and with the values of mass media—the values of propaganda, as set forth by Edward Bernays, the father of the public relations industry. Warhol's demolition of rigidly defined categories of art practice, which Duchamp accomplished by an abstemiously circumscribed output, followed instead Warhol's dictum, "Always leave them wanting less."

Duchamp signed cigars that his artist friends then smoked. Warhol would have had them encased in a vitrine.

Duchamp and Warhol are polar opposites in an important sense. Warhol, workaholic, motored by ravening ambition and sublimated, orgasmic pleasure in making things, happily produced as much as possible. Duchamp, imperturbably content to play chess, left art to its own devices and, more as a hobby than an all-summarizing statement, fussed with the same single, secret tableau to be viewed through a keyhole, when the spirit moved him, during twenty years of apparent indolence.

Despite the radical differences in their personalities and their backgrounds, they understood each other. Duchamp hadn't any anxious memories of poverty. He had been consistently undaunted, even amused, by rejection. Warhol, a passive-aggressive personality par excellence, regressed to infantile petulance when excluded from a group show, when he felt slighted or short-changed of the attention he demanded.

Warhol's capacious intellect was tweaked by the emotional affect of an eight-year-old. His insight and cunning deserve acknowledgment; so does his awesome immaturity. His knowingness about people matched his inability to sustain mature relationships. He encouraged the "inner children" of his entourage to act out their infantility on film.

His underlying kinship with Duchamp is the conceptual thread of art-as-idea that extends from the first through the second halves of the twentieth century. With both artists, the desire to "finish off art" is palpable. Yet neither could finish with art, for, as Duchamp noted, half the work of art is its reception, and the receivers invariably want more.

One may argue that Duchamp was, in his own term, "anti-retinal," whereas Warhol was all retinal. Warhol's retinal dimension, however, was a conceptual mystification of images, a kind of philosophic proof, demonstrated through seriality and repetition, a belief that all things can be made to resemble the same thing, not because of an artist's so-called signature style, but because a coherent attitude permeates his or her presentation of any subject.

Finally, it is their refusal to be "known," albeit in very different ways, that unites them. They both refined the idea of an impersonal art that reveals nothing about the person who made it, an art of detachment, a kind of industrial product much like any other. What the artist "felt" about his or her subject matter is irrelevant; the important thing is that the artist selected something in the world outside him/herself and isolated it from everything else, declared that it was "art" and therefore worthy of closer attention than other things. At the same time, this method of "art production" implicitly ratifies the idea than an artist is someone whose quality of attention exceeds that of other people, that anything such a person decides is worth examining qualifies as art—in effect, a quality control expert monitoring the ceaseless assembly line of objects and images in the world, not for the defective, but for the exceptionally resonant and meaningful.

Since this procedure really only requires the artist to convincingly carry it out once to qualify as an artist, as a special kind of historical spectator, it logically follows that the gesture, or demonstration, if sufficiently powerful and commanding enough attention, has to be performed only once for the artist's job to complete itself. Whatever the artist subsequently produces, in whatever medium, however different it seems to be from the original product, bears some seminal evidence of the same unique sensibility, or style, reflects the same unmistakable, quirky way of seeing the world, and qualifies as "valuable."

Warhol had the perspicacity to say that an artist really only paints one painting in his life. He did paint only one that turned the cultural world on its head.

TWO

A ndy Warhol's personal narrative is compelling because it contains elements of cherished American fantasies, the rags-to-riches, meritocratic payoff for unremitting hard work and obduracy—and because, at the apex of this dream come true, the dreamer gets shot several times with a handgun by someone on the far periphery of his realm. This part of the narrative has the more contemporary flavor of the official version of the Kennedy assassination: world's most important person killed by world's most insignificant person.

In 1968 Warhol was shot by a Factory hanger-on, one Valerie Solanas; she was a bit player in one of his films, *I, a Man*; the author of the infamous *SCUM Manifesto*, she had given Andy a script that had gotten lost in the Factory shuffle; she arrived at the Factory with a gun after failing to locate her publisher and intended target, Maurice Girodias, settling for Andy instead. Warhol survived Valerie Solanas's gunshot attack and went on producing things, even during his protracted recovery. Accounts of that time are typically ambiguous, insofar as he's said to have continued things he was working on and made no immediate changes in his living habits except as dictated by his medical condition. The shooting, however, is also cited as the event that changed everything in the Warhol cosmos, the moment when the party stopped, when the Factory became a conventional office and Warhol's artmaking became entirely about business.

The shooting occurred on June 3, just three days before the assassination of Robert Kennedy, which framed Andy's plight in a small lens, but the perception of Warhol's artistic activity, from outside at least, remained for several years more or less what it had been. The novel *a* appeared, *Blue Movie* was filmed; if the studio, relocated to Union Square, was no longer open house but a more recognizably conventional business setting, this facilitated procurement of advertising for *Interview* and the portrait commissions Warhol relied on during much of the 1970s to keep his shop running.

Andy got shot, he got scared, he got greedy, and he never waited for a fresh idea to slow down his production of art. And he became enamored of his evolving mutation into respectability. He had surrounded himself with colorfully marginal personalities, most of them harmless, but it only took one violent lunatic for Warhol to recognize the need to shed the crazies and cultivate the well-to-do and to tailor his career into a more buttoned-down, conventionally businesslike enterprise.

Warhol's near-death experience in 1968 and the ongoing toll it took on his body magnified his need for security. He grew up queer and impoverished, and the fear and insecurity he'd brazened his way through to become an icon in the world of images were suddenly manifested in physical violence that may have looked like a movie but certainly didn't feel like one. Almost all of Warhol's internal organs had been punctured or grazed by bullets, and he would have to hold his torso together with a corset for the rest of his life.

The stories America was telling itself about itself had become unsettling and contradictory by 1968. Martin Luther King and Robert Kennedy had been killed within a few months of each other. The expanding reach of public relations heightened a sense of nonexistence in those who weren't "known" to masses of strangers; the fate of strangers, and nameless people, was much at issue during the Vietnam War, but at least part of the momentum of the antiwar movement derived from the participation of media celebrities and famous writers.

The single most devastating lesson of the 1960s and early 1970s was that progressive institutional change in American society would not be permitted to happen. It took a long time for the lesson to sink in everywhere, and whether or not it has bearing on Warhol's eventual embrace of "Business Art," his work became the mirror of an unameliorated capitalist ethos, at ease with portrait commissions from the Shah of Iran and taped reflections of Imelda Marcos; making the world safe for Andy Warhol involved making Andy Warhol safe for the world.

THREE

The Warhol '70s began on a high, bright note. With the launching of Andy Warhol's *Interview* late in 1969 and the artist's prodigious portrait commission work, as Bob Colacello reports in *Holy Terror*, the '70s were a very good decade for Andy Warhol Enterprises in terms of profit and growing visibility. However, the rising monetary tide was mitigated by a decline in his artistic reputation; money was not able to purchase critical respect.

Many series of works after his Mao portraits, begun in 1972, were overlooked, or overshadowed, by the commissioned portraits he produced throughout the 1970s: Warhol's avidity about rousting up portrait commissions from anyone with the $25,000 to buy a portrait and the realms of wealth and privilege in which Warhol more and more exclusively spent his time were viewed by many critics and former members of Warhol's circle as a betrayal of a subversive practice, even a Marxist one; Warhol's harshest critics portrayed him as a sort of lapdog to the rich.

Warhol's art once again bifurcates, between commissioned work and subjects that "made a statement." In the 1970s, however, both kinds of work spelled Warhol, and a commissioned portrait, its subject reprocessed and cosmeticized into an idealization, became a Warhol painting, a lipstick trace of the person whose Polaroid image it was extracted from.

By mid-decade at the latest, most of Warhol's static visual work had become, in the opinion of many, static in every way. Too many of his commissioned portraits had a slapped-together and rebarbative ugliness, uncharacteristically lifeless blocks of color and thick smears of arbitrary brushwork, and the dazzling exceptions sometimes depicted subjects of widespread public odium, such as the Shah of Iran.

Moreover, the international peregrinations of Warhol, Fred Hughes, and Bob Colacello, the nightly revels
at Studio 54, and the reverentially recounted antics, in
Warhol's Diaries, of Liza, Truman, Halston, Diana
Vreeland, Bianca, Victor Hugo, and the second- and
third-string heiresses, princes, arms dealers, sons and
daughters of military dictators, millionettes and debu-
tantes, alienated Warhol's earlier, more bohemian following, who remained on the increasingly teeny fringes
of New York City, if they lived at all.

There were glamorous parties and happenings every
night where Andy Warhol's appearance was the ne plus
ultra of chic. There were many others where the entrance of Andy Warhol made a room fall practically
silent and his presence killed whatever spontaneous good
time the other guests had been having. People became
uneasily conscious of the Warhol stare, which intruded
the sensation of no longer being a guest at a party but
the unwilling object of hostile scrutiny in a morgue.

Not everyone loves the rich and privileged, and as
Punk became the reigning spirit of anarchy in a New
York City teetering on fiscal collapse, Warhol's ubiquity
at places like the Iranian embassy endeared him only to
those who lived on caviar and Champagne served in
gilded buckets, those who spent enough money on
baubles to support several African nations.

The Warhol embrace of the ruling class was natural to him: having never been middle-class, he'd gone directly from penury to affluence and fame. But Warhol's transition from profound superficiality and transgression to the cultivation of the rich and powerful sanded the edges off his charisma and, for many, turned him into a self-parody and an ambulatory corpse. At the end of the '70s, *Interview*'s drooling adoration of the Reagans, the Warhol clique's infatuation with "the return of style and elegance" to the White House, and the implicit endorsement of the cutthroat economics and further disparities between rich and poor the Reagan Revolution represented didn't help matters.

This is not an entirely fair or justified appraisal of Warhol's work during the era in question—what he made wasn't invariably awful, it was almost always eye-catching and droll, occasionally it still carried some charge of surprise, and scattered throughout his later production were occasional works of real brilliance—but a reflection on how a substantial segment of New York's fermenting new cultural mixtures and many earlier, approving critical eyes now saw him. And as the city became much more gruesomely divided between the monied and the moneyless, struggling artists and lavishly rewarded ones, Warhol was implemental in demolishing what remained of sustainable marginality.

The movers and shakers whose fiestas he ornamented were the same people gutting ethnically mixed neighborhoods, eradicating affordable housing, suburbanizing New York into a bland expanse of generic malls, rebarbarizing Manhattan's center into a playground for the ultrarich, and shoving the sources of its cultural wealth, its struggling, talented young fleeing provincial suffocation, out to the boroughs and beyond.

FOUR

A decade separates the revered Marilyn from Mao in the Warhol canon. The paintings of Monroe and other media stars made one kind of sense, as the secular "saints" of a culture infatuated with and shaped by celebrity worship. Warhol was depicting figures whose most widely disseminated images and backstories of personal tragedy carried all sorts of meanings for the American public who adored them; their enshrinement by Warhol had an emotional logic for the general public and a wealth of exegetical resonance for critics. It's difficult to recall the impact of Warhol's Maos and to say with certainty how most people reacted to them. It was a convulsive era, the nasty end of "the counterculture," and a kind of slash-and-burn political frenzy had set in:

Maoism, at many universities, had become a last-ditch ideological extremity that proposed simple, absolute answers to impossibly complicated questions, and perhaps much of its appeal was that it was doomed from the start.

Warhol's Pop Art "statement," as he was wont to call it, dates from the pre–*Campbell's Soup Can* comic strip panel paintings of Superman, Nancy, Dick Tracy, et al.—all of which have inspired a wealth of fascinating interpretations—to the decisive "slap in America's face" of the soup cans and other commonplace supermarket products, through the movie star icons, the "death period," the flowers, and the Mao series.

With the *Soup Cans* in mind as the paintings that broke down the barriers and "made the world safe for Andy Warhol," the Pop meditation on celebrity, as distinct from Warhol's later depictions of the celebrated, might be bracketed with Marilyn Monroe at one end and Mao Tse-tung at the other.

Monroe epitomizes, incarnates, embodies "stardom": likewise, the Monroe paintings return us to Warhol's childhood fascination with movie magazines, studio stills, the autographed fan pix he sent away for and treasured, as well as his fixé on the received image, the preextant photograph.

Stardom has always been disseminated through photography—motion photography, news photographs, publicity stills, "mechanical reproduction" in all its forms. The concept of stardom assumes a plurality of stars, an assembly line of camera-perfected faces, a Hindu multiplicity of gods or idols. Stars are unique; stars are interchangeable. They age. They wear out their welcome. As with all technological commodities, the accelerated velocity of product redundancy has shortened the life span and lessened the iconic resonance of stardom: anyone who watches movies made now can name at least three or more almost indistinguishable actors and actresses, or more than likely cannot name them correctly. To compound the problem, most of them are very good actors, though we wouldn't call them "stars."

The stardom of Old Hollywood had far more staying power and infinitely fewer actors who closely resembled each other. Warhol chose Marilyn Monroe because she was, unmistakably, Marilyn Monroe (and she had just died, becoming "forever Marilyn," in an unfortunate sense, as she looked in 1953); Elvis because no other Elvis existed; and Liz because, with the exception of Faye Dunaway, Liz Taylor was the last true Hollywood movie star (and at the time she was expected to die of pneumonia in London any minute).

What the Warhol Maos seem to say, at least to the radically minded in 1972, was that stardom in the Amer-

ican sense was rapidly losing iconographic resonance—
that celebrities were, for that matter, interchangeable by
nature, and that it was plausible, maybe even expedi-
tious, for a nation of millions to have one single identifi-
able celebrity ("Out of many, one"). The famous Warhol
combine photograph *Crowd* (1963) evokes the horror of
a world packed like a sardine can with anonymous indi-
viduals. But given Warhol's unswerving predilection for
"what is," *Crowd* also prompts the question, What else
is there?

Celebrity, even individuation, may be a chimera;
Zen teaches that there is no me, no you, no self. One absurdist response to this nothingness could be the secular
monotheism of a single figure as the representative
ideal of the entire human species. Warhol's Mao incarnates this: he constantly sought the simplest solution to
any aesthetic problem, and there, in Mao, he found it.
But like many Warhol solutions, this one was comic, de-
flationary, and monumentally cheeky.

In many of the painting's variants Mao looks like
the madame of a seedy brothel in Shanghai, in others a
transvestite waitress in regulation Mao jacket. And the
phrase "warts and all" has been literally applied. Both
the problem and the solution of "celebrity" were as il-
lusory as the "self," and Warhol's Marilyn-into-Mao
conveyed the insouciance of a globally significant goof.

Capitalism's supreme enemy became a capitalist collectible. Still, the Warhol Mao is somehow the last vestige of celebrity worship in the old sense, the last icon that could represent all icons.

Celebrity worship was no longer an epiphanic experience for Warhol: it was a business, and a business contingent on rapid turnover of inventory. *Interview* magazine, which began by featuring, amid a certain amount of dross, long interviews with the truly famous, devolved into a fanzine for the three-minute attention span: one month's "Interman" and "Viewgirl" became next month's birdcage liner, and after Warhol's death it became a catalog of show biz trash and ephemera, ready for the birdcage before it hit the stands.

FIVE

As the decade wore on, there was more chaff than wheat produced in Andy's mill, and a great many discarded former familiars were eager to denigrate the artist himself and anything he exhibited. Some people once associated with Warhol felt betrayed by him, financially cheated, lied to, deceived, ripped off. Others expected the celebrity he conferred on them to transform their lives, and in most cases it didn't wreak much improvement on their original situations. Others still moved on and put the Factory days, or years, behind them. Some of Warhol's friends had always kept a distance from the vortex of the Factory.

As people who spent several years in Andy's orbit have observed, it's impossible to tell the story of what went on at the Factory with any real authority, because the ever-shifting scene and its hierarchies of favor and disfavor were all about ambiguity, and everybody has a different version of it. The most an outsider can say is that Warhol contrived a social sphere in which a lot of viciousness got played out, where a high mortality rate came with the circles he exploited in his films and incorporated into his entourage. Survivors of the Age of Silver tend to express ambiguous feelings about Warhol, love and hatred in varying quantities.

Warhol could confer celebrity. He could not endow anyone with a durable sense of self, and it may be that those who confused celebrity with identity were the most vulnerable and likely to crash and burn. In the period before he was shot by Valerie Solanas, Warhol collected a large, ever-shifting entourage of vividly unstable personalities who, often desperately, needed to attach themselves to a charismatic figure (some would say a father figure). Their proximity to Warhol gave them a kind of status in the world, membership in the media circus; appearing in front of his camera allowed many of them to play out self-destructive behavior and confuse it with the recognition of talent, success, fame; the psychologically neediest of these sometimes brilliant but seriously damaged personalities often ended their days in suicide and drug overdoses.

SIX

Warhol's celebrity as an image is matched by his total disappearance, as a person, behind his work. Nobody knew him, according to many old Factory hands who saw him every day for years. The unavoidable conclusion is that Warhol didn't want to be known. He wanted to be seen, which isn't at all the same thing. Being seen was an important part of his job.

Warhol's transcription of all the data of the everyday, his preservation of junk mail, invitations, and all manner of things that strayed into his ken as "time capsules," reflects the heightened sense of ephemerality that has accompanied successive technological interventions into everyone's everyday life. The velocity of contemporary urban life generates an unmanageable quantity of unwelcome, distracting ephemera, of messages competing for attention that can never be deciphered, much less answered: Warhol's time capsules are an archaeology of surplus information, and their ongoing "excavation" is both revelatory and absurd, arguably making the artist both more palpable and more elusively absent.

Warhol's best works speak for themselves—or rather, don't speak for anything, since theirs is the language of silence the artist cultivated and arguably perfected. If Warhol had followed his own ukase of silence, his art might well have achieved an aura of mystery that would have rendered it more expressive, more moving, more emotive, more beautiful, more disruptive.

The reality, however, is that this sphinx of silence and cunning never shut up about himself, his work, his memories, his reflections, his skin problems, his sex problems, his eating habits, his techniques for figuring out other people, his refusal to check his shopping bags when he entered a supermarket, his infatuation with money, his admiration of Diana Vreeland, his actors, his publicity, his triumphs and failures. If Warhol wasn't crazy about talking (though he was, you only had to hear him on the phone to realize he was a champion blabbermouth), he had an authentic mania for writing and publishing everything he wouldn't say in a face-to-face conversation, or even on the phone.

Almost all of Warhol's books are entertainments, literary vaudevilles. The voice is never quite the same voice, and it never sounds entirely like Andy's voice; like everything about him, the books produce an ambiguity that heightens interest while undermining any certainty about what's true, what's a put-on, and who exactly wrote which parts of it. When one book rakes over the same story told in another book, each relates it differently, shifts the emphasis or alters details; one book uses pseudonyms, another the real names of the characters, and Warhol claims different thoughts and opinions about the same people; some extended passages are partially fictionalized, whereas others attempt to adhere closely to the facts. They can be read many times without turning stale, even though second or third readings tell us nothing new. Warhol's books are neither trash nor literature. They're a sort of verbal Pop Art.

The magnum opus is *The Andy Warhol Diaries*, a day-to-day account, delivered via telephone to Pat Hackett, of Warhol's activities the day and night before. Originally it had been conceived as a way to track expenses, as Warhol had been audited by the IRS every year after donating a poster to George McGovern's presidential campaign. (It featured a ghoulishly colored picture of Richard Nixon with "Vote McGovern" scrawled below it.)

The Diaries is markedly unlike Warhol's other books. Although it became an immediate best-seller and on every page drops embarrassing disclosures about the secret lives of the people Warhol hung around with between November 1976 and February 1987, it's unpleasant reading from page 1 and rather quickly becomes nauseating and almost unbearable. Warhol brings his usually hidden opinions about people, and what seems an unintentionally fullish exposure of his own personality, into the open.

The Andy Warhol Diaries, unlike the revved-up, slapstick spirit and absurdist humor of his books of memoirs, is lively with proper names and lifeless in its overdetailed accounts of Warhol's travels and his variegated activities in New York during the period it covers. It tells you everything you never wanted to know about the people Warhol regularly saw and partied with in those years—which is more or less anything.

Warhol condenses the noteworthy moments of a fast-motion circuit of parties, openings, celebrity visits to the Factory, and what feels like an eon of nightly carousing at Studio 54. Behind all this frenetic activity, behind all the compulsive shopping Warhol does walking partway from his uptown home to Union Square, behind the jokes, behind the drugs everybody—except Andy, of course—ingests in near-lethal quantities, behind the movie stars giving blow jobs to waiters in the balcony at 54, behind the telegraphically concise background histories of numerous recurring characters, and behind the encyclopedic coverage of the artful strategies Fred and Bob and the others devised to secure portrait commissions—the book is surely as long as *Moby-Dick*, or only fractionally shorter—behind all of this the reader sees, a little too clearly, an ambulatory wig whose wow, gee whiz, and golly act has gone stale as a month-old doughnut.

Warhol seems not to notice it, but his vision of the world has almost entirely replaced the world that existed before he began indicting boredom, apathy, emotional emptiness, partial autism, and ugliness by exhibiting these negative qualities in his own persona. Since Warhol's death, that vision has accelerated its spread over all of America and much of the developed world, like the map invented by Borges that grows large enough to physically coincide with the entire territory it charts.

SEVEN

Warhol may have sometimes entertained the wish to be a private person, but few Americans have ever been less so. During the time when he incarnated the ne plus ultra of cool, the aphorisms and observations he coined, the books he published, the magazine with his John Hancock over the title, conveyed a richly whimsical way of seeing things, but these things were also given weight and taken seriously by successive waves of fans/followers/devotees and too many people trying to dredge a role model out of a Dumpster. Part sphinx, part Svengali, with a bit of Simon Legree and Uriah Heep thrown into the mix, Warhol, his writings, his movies, his paintings, and *Interview* magazine held a surprisingly widespread, nervous-making sway over how Americans felt about the country they lived in, how they reacted to new technologies, how they thought about themselves, and how they treated other people.

Whether the result of inattention, passivity, a virulent resurgence of fears instilled in his childhood, anti-intellectualism and the closely related aversion to value judgments, intoxicating proximity to power, creative exhaustion, a late-developing failure to effectively control things within his realm, disorientingly rapid revisions of the culture's structural mechanisms—which he'd formerly grasped, in every particular, with something close to omniscience—or the convergence of all these elements within a brief span, Andy Warhol, who'd become "Andy Warhol" years earlier, was increasingly perceived, after the mid-1970s, as "the former Andy Warhol."

If he had always looked spectral and pallid and strategically exaggerated his natural reticence and played up his own absurdity and unlikelihood, in the period covered by his *Diaries* Warhol's celebrity had already outlasted his fame; in the new world evolving around him, the significant difference between the two was something Americans were becoming mentally and morally unequipped to recognize.

chapter seven

PORTRAIT OF THE IMAGE AS "IMPORTANT" ARTIST

ONE

WARHOL CHANGED AMERICAN CULTURE PRO-foundly. He brought its underlying nature into stark visibility. The paradox is that we were, and are, reluctant to look at the culture we have, its imperialist presumptions, its incredible ugliness, the direction it's taken, and where it's leading us, and to recognize Warhol as the weather vane of its condition, the prophet of its inevitable endgame.

Making the world safe for Andy Warhol was a proj-ect that expanded as it absorbed territory: the *Soup Can* paintings can be seen as the first substantial foray in Warhol's conquest of America, an emptying-out and leveling of its contents and a celebration of its "democratic" offering of the same things to everybody. Warhol liked to remark that a movie star could drink a Coke, and so could you. He also said that the Queen of England couldn't get a better hot dog at Yankee Stadium than anyone else.

There was something disingenuous about Andy Warhol's notion of democracy, which he defined as access to consumer goods of identical quality. However, this consistently fails to acknowledge the disparity of wealth distribution that sharply separates "access" from purchasing power. Instead, it extols the accelerated technological production of "choices" between essentially identical objects—specifically, aside from "personal products," cybernetic devices that surface first as novelties and quickly acquire a ubiquity and psycho-social necessity, the universal modifications in the fabric of daily life that transform novelty items into utilitarian objects that we then have no choice about owning: computers, cell phones, answering machines, DVD players, television sets, and a gamut of other things that alter the temporal dimension in radical ways, bringing us ever closer to the usurpation of consciousness by our incremental transformation into automata.

Warhol anticipated this equalization of people by their dependence on the same habits of consumption: of goods, information, and modes of transpersonal exchange. He drastically changed the content and meaning of celebrity and revealed its transience and redundancy, as well as its appeal to the mass unconscious Walter Benjamin identifies in his discussion of cinema and photography in "The Work of Art in the Age of Mechanical Reproduction." Mimesis, in Warhol's itinerary, ultimately achieved parity with what it depicted. *The Warhol Diaries* records nonstop social encounters with Jackie Kennedy, Liz Taylor, and other people Warhol painted when they were unattainably distant signifiers of celebrity.

Warhol changed the meaning of the recognizable. To say he became what he beheld isn't quite accurate. Often what he beheld became him. The Campbell's soup can became Warhol. Marilyn Monroe became Warhol. Or more correctly, an image of Marilyn Monroe became inextricably linked with Warhol, and a Campbell's soup can became foremost a signifier of Warhol and only secondarily a soup can.

In Warhol's work, mimesis operates like a value-neutral virus leaping boundaries, from a bloody car crash to oversaturated flowers on wallpaper patterns of a cow, selected from an elaborate photographic selection of cows (each originary image annotated with a written description) for its quintessence of bovinity; from the *Mona Lisa* to Mao; from cocks and asses to skulls and shadows: it's all material, it's all the same, and it's all grist for the mill of technological reproduction and superficial "beautification" and consumption.

Warhol beatified the ordinary and rendered the sensational banal through serial repetition of its imagery. He didn't simply level the playing field of art; he flattened it, rendering the work of art as a pricey commodity.

TWO

Warhol's celebrity never went into eclipse, but his status as an artist passed through a fairly long dark period, much of which coincides with the period covered by *The Warhol Diaries*. The negative impression Warhol's work of the 1970s left on American art mavens and many other people is partly deserved, for the same reason Bob Colacello cites for the artist's abandonment of the Factory lifestyle: he got older. Great works of art don't come pouring out of anyone incessantly over the course of a career; an artist is blessedly lucky if he hits a long winning streak once or twice in his lifetime, as Warhol did between 1962 and 1964.

When Warhol painted the *Soup Cans*, the culture was in need of works of art that weren't intended to "say" anything, to "represent" anything. Warhol's paintings were simply what they were. The *Campbell's Soup Cans* weren't the "manifest content" of some "latent content" behind them. They didn't need—and clearly Warhol didn't wish for them—to be parsed in the way Freud analyzed his patients' dreams. In 1962 Warhol's work had the singular virtue of resisting the kind of otiose, convoluted readings that Clement Greenberg and other critics injected into Abstract Expressionism. There was nothing to read into Warhol's works. Indeed, as Warhol correctly thought, they were as close to nothing as a picture of something could be.

They startled, they shocked, they pissed people off. They also refreshed the sense of surprise and unmediated pleasure of looking at beautiful visual objects without requiring them to "mean" anything. All they revealed, really, was that a soup can grabbed off a supermarket shelf could be beautiful exactly as it was, in all its monumentalized banality.

In the many years that have passed since Warhol's *Soup Cans* appeared in the Ferus Gallery, American culture has undergone drastic changes. The paintings themselves still look fresh, still jump out at the viewer and leave a tactile afterimage on the eyes. In the globalized art market, the aesthetic blandishments of any works of art seem less significant than their exchange value: we may well love what something looks like, agree with, puzzle over, or dispute what a work of art seems to "say" (if it seems to "say" anything), yet we're more than likely, first and foremost, to be interested in what its monetary value is purported to be, in some cases how much it cost to construct and exhibit it, and how its producer, a celebrity manufactured by the corporate machinery of the art world, is faring in the circuitry of capitalism.

THREE

It's often said that Marcel Duchamp and Andy Warhol were the two most important artists of the twentieth century. The status of "important" is usually thought to confer exalted significance on an artist or on his or her work, though it does no such thing. "Important" can connote either the baleful or the salubrious, describe a disastrous event as well as a fortuitous one. The word itself doesn't distinguish a bankruptcy from a windfall. Moreover, it can describe opposite values or effects at the same time.

An important artist can be a good or a bad one, or sometimes a good one, sometimes a bad one, or good for a time and bad later on, and vice versa. In this specific context of culture and what kind of culture a society has, and what kind of art that culture generates in that society, whether an "important" work of art is good, bad, or indifferent may very well be an irrelevance. If we substitute "influential" for "important," we come closer to understanding why Andy Warhol remains a living presence in world culture and how Andy Warhol changed the culture of the United States. "Influential," too, can denote two opposite things simultaneously.

At the risk of mystifying Warhol instead of rendering him transparent, it's possible that his importance was, and is, that his art and life changed what Americans consider important. Important, that is to say, in an obviously limited sphere. Warhol's achievements and failures belong to the realm of artistic culture, or, if one wants to conflate them, "culture," period—and it would be absurd to claim that a series of paintings of Campbell's soup cans, in and of themselves, transformed our world. Nowhere in this little book have I attempted to make this claim; it's simply my belief that, among the myriad works of art produced in America before and after (including other seminal works of Pop Art), the *Soup Cans* have a pivotal importance in the transformation of artistic culture from a somewhat hermetic and highly elitist microcosm to a more populist and accessible territory.

Even this is disputable, of course; minus the *Soup Cans*, even minus Warhol, in America and other advanced societies, given the metastatic spread of mass communications and the evolution of public relations into a globalized phenomenon, "movements" and trends, artists-as-celebrities, and art, of whatever kind, as a global commodity would undoubtedly have produced the "art economy" as it currently exists.

On the other hand, retrospectively, the *Soup Can* series and the Warhol phenomenon look historically inevitable. (The past always does.) They clarified in a powerful way what the true underpinnings of American culture were: commodity, consumption, and celebrity worship. To take a purely negative view, one could add velocity, vicariousness, and instant obsolescence, the erasure of historical memory, and the three-second attention span induced by mass media, but one has to go way beyond Andy Warhol to identify the multiple causes of these baleful phenomena.

A more neutral and arguably more positive way of thinking about Warhol is this: at least in that hyperproductive period of great works that began with the *Soup Cans* and concluded, in many assessments, in 1968, the year when he was almost fatally shot by Valerie Solanas, Warhol created a body of work, a milieu, and a mythology so resonant and alluring that many of the world's finest artists, of all kinds, who've emerged in subsequent decades would readily acknowledge that Warhol's multifaceted enterprise "gave permission" for them to exploit new technologies, to push into otherwise unimaginable aesthetic terrain, to create invaluable critique and observation of the society around them. Indeed, a list of such artists would be impossibly long to compile and would hardly be limited to Americans. In this sense, yes, Andy Warhol and his *Soup Cans* have had incalculable influence throughout the world—the world of art and aesthetics, the world of ideas about what ought to be preserved for posterity.

The world itself is a different story.

ACKNOWLEDGMENTS

I would like to thank the staff of the Andy Warhol Foundation for the Visual Arts in New York and the Andy Warhol Museum in Pittsburgh for their generous help in supplying me with research materials and with space to work on the initial version of this book, and Dena Santoro for advice and assistance on streamlining the final text.

NOTES

CHAPTER ONE

1. Simon Callow, *Orson Welles*, vol. 1, *The Road to Xanadu* (New York: Penguin Books, 1997), pp. 420–421.

2. Jamie Warhola, private letter to the author, June 17, 2007.

CHAPTER TWO

1. Alice Goldfarb Marquis, *Art Czar: The Rise and Fall of Clement Greenberg* (Boston: MFA Publications, 2006), p. 96.

2. Frances Stonor Saunders, *The Cultural Cold War: The CIA and the World of Arts and Letters* (New York: New Press, 1999), p. 253.

3. Dwight D. Eisenhower, "Freedom in the Arts," Museum of Modern Art twenty-fifth anniversary address, October 19, 1954, reprinted in *Museum of Modern Art Bulletin* (1954), quoted in Saunders, *The Cultural Cold War*, p. 272.

4. Saunders, *The Cultural Cold War*, p. 263.

5. Victor Bockris, *The Life and Death of Andy Warhol* (New York: Bantam Books, 1989), pp. 95–96.

6. Simon Watney, "Queer Andy," in *Pop Out/Queer Warhol*, edited by Jennifer Doyle, Jonathan Flatley, and José Esteban Muñoz (Durham: Duke University Press, 1996), p. 29.

7. Andy Warhol and Pat Hackett, *POPism: The Warhol Sixties* (New York: Harcourt, 1980), p. 15.

8. Bockris, *The Life and Death of Andy Warhol*, p. 98.

CHAPTER FOUR

1. Bob Colacello, *Holy Terror: Andy Warhol Close Up* (New York: HarperCollins, 1990), p. 28.

2. Eric Shanes, *Warhol: The Life and Masterworks* (New York: Parkstone Press, 2004), p. 41.

3. Quoted in Heiner Bastian, *AW* (MOCA catalog; London: Tate Publishing, 2001, reprinted by the Museum of Contemporary Art, Los Angeles, 2002), p. 58.

4. Jules Langsner, "Los Angeles Letter," *Art International* (September 1962): 49, reprinted in *POP ART: A Critical History*, edited by Steven Henry Madoff (Berkeley: University of California Press, 1997), p. 33.

5. Michael Fried, "New York Letter," *Art International* (December 20, 1962): 57, reprinted in Madoff, *Pop Art*, p. 267.

6. Donald Judd, "In the Galleries: Andy Warhol," *Arts* (January 1963): 49, reprinted in Madoff, *Pop Art*, p. 268.

7. Philip Larratt-Smith, interview with John Baldessari, in *Andy Warhol: Mr. America* (Bogota, Colombia: Museo de Arte del Banco de la Republica, 2009), p. 266.

CHAPTER FIVE

1. Kenneth Goldsmith, ed., *I'll Be Your Mirror: The Selected Andy Warhol Interviews* (New York: Carroll & Graf, 2004), p. 96.

2. Mary Woronov, *Swimming Underground* (Boston: Journey Editions, 1995), p. 152.

INDEX